THE GRACE OF GOD IN JEWISH TRADITION

Richard S. Hanson

EMText
San Francisco

Library of Congress Cataloging-in-Publication Data

Hanson, Richard S.
    The grace of God in Jewish tradition / Richard Simon Hanson.
       p.   cm.
    Includes bibliographical references (p.).
    ISBN 0-7734-1932-2
    1. God (Judaism) 2. Judaism--Doctrines. 3. Judaism--Essence,
genius, nature. 4. Judaism--Relations--Christianity.
5. Christianity and other religions--Judaism. I. Title.
 BM610.H36   1993
 296.3'11--dc20

                                          92-42128
                                            CIP

Editorial Inquiries:

Mellen Research University Press
534 Pacific Avenue
San Francisco
CA 94133

Order Fulfillment:

The Edwin Mellen Press
P.O. Box 450
Lewiston, NY 14092
USA

Printed in the United States of America

TABLE OF CONTENTS

Acknowledgements

Thanks to various colleagues in various places for encouragement on this project, to A. Thomas Kraabel of Luther College, Eric and Carol Meyers of Duke University, Harold Kasimov of Grinnel College, A. Joseph Everson of California Lutheran and Menahem Mor of Creighton. For help with the logistics and production of the manuscript, thanks to Melissa Halling Amundson, my student assistant, to my colleague John Sieber and, for helping greatly with last minute problems, Deb Shook.

INTRODUCTION

I am not Jewish and, like many non-Jewish people, I was brought up with a fair dose of anti-Jewishness fed into my system. Oh, not that vicious kind of anti-Semitism that produces pogroms and such. Only something more subtle. The folks who raised me did not hate or even resent Jewish people. They only regarded them as a people who had somehow missed the way, who had rejected Christ when the time for acceptance was theirs and whose existence was somehow corrupt ever since.

I was not very old when I learned the meaning of Jew in such a line as "Don't let 'im Jew y' down." The occasion was the announced appearance of a scrap iron dealer in our rural neighborhood. My grandfather, who was a good-hearted, genuinely amiable person, said it. It was not that he had anything against Jewish people as such. He had merely inherited the notion that Jewish merchants and peddlers were not to be trusted and drove a hard bargain in business. Therefore, when he left the premises for the day and his son and son-in-law in charge of the farm, he gave them that final warning regarding the scrap iron they would try to get the itinerant dealer to buy.

In my religious education and in church I was taught that the Jews were those who opposed Jesus, who saw to his crucifixion, who were damned because they rejected Christ. They were the "people of the law." They did not understand such things as God's forgiveness in Christ or the Gospel. They were ignorant of God's grace.

As I listen to the voices around me today and read the popular Christian literature of our time, I notice a great amount of that same attitude and point of view that shaped me in my growing. I observe that the majority of Christians still think of Jewish people as at least outside the realm of grace if not actually damned for being Jewish. Those who live by stereotypes still have Jewish people stereotyped as a rejected race.

It has now been quite some time since I first recognized this about my fellow Christians. For that reason I have spent a quarter of a century teaching their offspring about the ways, history and thinking of Jewish people. As a college professor I have tried to educate at least a few young Christians out of this naive view of Jews and Judaism. In the process I have come to see with greater and greater precision where it is that Christians are most blind to what Jews experience, teach and practice and out of that understanding I am now embarking on some attempts to correct Christian vision at certain points. It is my hope that I can help my fellow Christians to understand things they have not understood before and, with that increased understanding, move into meaningful dialogue and fellowship with Jewish people.

There are some points at which Christianity and Judaism appear to be obviously different. One such point is the matter of the Messiah. Overlooking the fact that messianism is an idea held commonly by Jews and Christians and therefore a matter that could be more binding than divisive, most people have considered Jesus to be the point of separation. Christians typically assume that "the question of Jesus" is the question of all questions and all too many Jews are willing to fall for that misconception. And from that misconception proceed a number of others including the common Christian assumption that Jews know or experience nothing of divine grace.

It is my purpose to sidestep what has heretofore been considered the central question and, by examining some of the matters that relate to it, to demonstrate that Jews and Christians are far more alike than different in their experience of life and in their religious convictions. Here I have chosen to examine the concept of divine grace in the Jewish tradition. Should this prove to be helpful or successful, I hope to pursue other themes.

Christians typically think they have a monopoly on the grace of God. The very word is central to the Christian vocabulary in a way that is not so in other religious traditions. It is what Jesus and the Gospel are all about, a Christian would say. It was the grace of God that Jesus revealed and it is, in one way or another, only through Jesus that grace is available. In the Catholic wing of the Church, that availability is sacramental. For Protestants, it is typically through "the preaching of the Word," by which we are "saved." As far as most Christians are concerned, those who do not "know," "accept" or "believe in" Jesus or those who are not "baptized into Christ" are surely ignorant of God's grace and outside the realm of its benefits.

The grace of God is the theme of some of the greatest of Christian hymnody. Whether in the chorales of European tradition or the gospel songs of America, it is strong and central. A perfect example of it is the American folk hymn with the following text.

> Amazing grace, how sweet the sound
> that saved a wretch like me!
> I once was lost but now am found,
> was blind but now I see.
>
> 'Twas grace that taught my heart to fear
> and grace my fears relieved.
> How precious did that grace appear
> the hour I first believed!
>
> Through many dangers, toils and snares
> I have already come.
> 'Tis grace has brought me safe thus far
> and grace will lead me home.
>
> The Lord has promised good to me;
> his Word my hope secures.
> He will my shield and portion be
> as long as life endures.

It is of course true that each of the Christian traditions has its own favorite language for speaking of divine grace. Among Catholics and those most closely allied to the Catholic tradition, that language is the language of the sacraments. Among Protestants it is more common to identify it with Scripture and scriptural phrases. Quoting such a passage as that of Paul's Letter to the Ephesians, 2:8, is a typically Protestant way to speak of it: For by grace you have been saved through faith; and this is not of your own doing, it is the gift of God (RSV). Recitation of Scripture and "preaching of the Word" are the language of Protestant Christianity.

Here I am going to make no attempt to describe or explain the varieties of Christian comprehensions of divine grace. I only remind the reader that it is a primary concept to all Christians and that it is, therefore, a matter of great concern whether there be an understanding of it in Judaism or among Jewish people. It will be my assertion that there is, indeed, a rich understanding and experience of it in Jewish tradition. The word "grace" itself will not occur commonly in Jewish speech or religious literature, to be sure, for it is a word born out of the Latin language. It will be in other words that the concept is embedded. But embedded it is. From the very traditions and language of the Bible out of which the Christian vocabulary sprang to Jewish religious or devotional literature of our day, the concept is alive and important. In this short work I hope to demonstrate that this is so and how it is so.

THE GRACE OF SHABBAT

There is a way in which shabbat (Sabbath) epitomizes the Jewish understanding of the grace of God. In the traditional orthodox conception of it, shabbat is more than the day set aside from the rest of the week for the worship of God. In the traditional orthodox understanding, shabbat is actually considered a gift from God. An anecdote from eastern European tradition illustrates this. It is a story I came across in E. E. Millgram's book, SABBATH: THE DAY OF DELIGHT. The anecdote is titled "The Sabbath of the Poor." Millgram has recounted it as follows.[1]

> Six days in the week Shmulik the rag-picker lives like a dog. But on the eve of the Sabbath all is changed in his house. The walls are whitewashed, the house is cleaned; a new cloth shines on the table, and the rich and yellow bread, a joy to the eyes, rests thereon. The candles burn in their copper candlesticks, burnished for the Sabbath; and a smell of good food goes out the oven, where the dishes are covered. All week long the mother of the house has been black as coal; today her face is resplendent, a white kerchief is tied on her head, and spirit of grace has breathed upon her. The little girls, with bare feet, have come back from the bath; their hair is coiled in tresses; they linger in the corners of the room; by their faces it may be seen that they are waiting, joyous hearted for those whom they love.
>
> "Gut Shabbos," says Shmulik, as he enters; and he looks with love on his wife and his children, and his face beams. "Gut Shabbos," says Moishele, his son, loudly, and he too enters hurriedly, like one who is full of good tidings, and eager to spread them. And to and from in the house the father and son go,

singing, with pleasant voices, the Shalom 'Alekem songs that greet the invisible angels that come into every Jewish house when the father returns from the house of prayer on the eve of Sabbath.

The rag-picker is no longer a dog; today he has a new soul. It is Shabbos, and Shmulik is the son of a king. He says the kiddush over the wine, and he sits down at the table. His wife is on his right, and his children are around them. They dip their spoons into the dish, to take a little soup, a piece of meat, a fragment of fish, of barley, or of the other good things they know nothing of during the week. The children carry these dainties to their lips with their five fingers, so that they may lose nothing of them. They eat carefully, as attentive to their food as the squirrel at the top of the tree, when he crunches a nut between his teeth and all his mind and body are concentrated on the act . . .

Now Shmulik clears his throat and begins to intone a song of the Sabbath. "Beautiful and holy is the Sabbath day." And his voice becomes stronger as he goes on to the Ma Yafit, and sings of the weary who find rest, and of the wild river Sambatyon, which is tumultuous six days of the week, and on the seventh rests from its rage. "Sambatyon, Sambatyon, wild with haste every day." Sambatyon ... is not Sambatyon Israel? All week long Israel runs from place to place. When the Sabbath day comes he pauses, and rests; and on the eve of the Sabbath there is no more sadness and no more sighing.

As Shmulik and the storyteller understood it, Sabbath was a gift. It was a day of freedom in a world of many restrictions, a day that permitted him to realize and celebrate his aspirations. It was a time of refreshment and renewal, a time given by God and written into the very order of creation.

Among some pious Jews Sabbath has actually been personified and regarded as a welcome guest to be taken as the very ambassadress of divine grace. Her approach is the approach of an intermediary, one who leaves us but one step removed from the very Presence. This somewhat naive but profound conviction is expressed in what may be the most well known of all Jewish folk hymns, in the song that is known as *lekhah dodi*. Here is an approximate translation of its text.

Come, my beloved, to meet a bride. Let us welcome the face of Shabbat. Enter in peace, O diadem of

your lord, in happiness and rejoicing, in the midst of
the faithful of the people chosen. Enter, O bride!
Let us welcome the face of Shabbat.

One must not take this too literally, of course. In the realm of religious
experience or religious vocabulary the most meaningful language is the language
of symbolism. I have worshipped with Jewish people who actually turn as a
single body to face the doorway when they sing this song to the bride and some
of them may have imagined a stately and beautiful woman walking through the
door, but the imaginary woman is not the reality of the occasion. The reality is
an experience that may be akin to a man's experience of a lovely bride. She is
the renewal produced by divine grace. If you will permit the use of more
symbolic language, "she" is a foretaste of the messianic age, of the glorious
consummation of *Olam ha-Bah*.

I rather think, in fact, that a pious Jew's experience of Queen Sabbath is
essentially the same as the pious Christian's experience of Christ in the
Eucharist.

Imagination is a wonderful gift. It permits such responses to the reality
as this hymn quoted in Eisenstein's HERITAGE OF MUSIC (p. 167).[2]

For love of thee my chalice I raise,
Welcome, O Sabbath, beloved of days.

How sweet it is, between day and night,
To glimpse Sabbath's face, aglow with light.
Bring apples and dainties for her delight.
Sing out her praise, sing roundelays,
Welcome, O Sabbath, beloved of days.

Love songs I sing, Sabbath my bride,
Love songs to thee, my joy and my pride.
Come to the feast, the door's open wide,
Let the lights blaze, with love I gaze,
Welcome, O Sabbath, beloved of days.

To Israel this day brings rest and release,
O Sabbath of peace, O Sabbath of peace.
God bade us cherish thee, long ago on Sinai's height,
To make of thee a day of rest, a day of light,
To spread a joyous feast, dainties rare for thy delight,
O Sabbath of peace, O Sabbath of peace.

A comparison of typical Christian hymns of response to the Eucharist
reveals that something very similar, if not the same, is going on. To sincerely
express oneself through either of these texts is to confess a confrontation with

something that is best called divine grace. The worshipper has experienced renewal, which may be the very purpose of devout worship.

> For the bread which you have broken,
> for the wine which you have poured,
> for the words which you have spoken,
> now we give you thanks, O Lord.

> By this promise that you love us,
> by your gift of peace restored,
> by your call to heav'n above us,
> hallow all our lives, O Lord.

> With the saints who now adore you
> seated at our Father's board,
> may the church still waiting for you
> keep love's tie unbroken, Lord.
> (Text by Louis F. Benson,[3]
> 1855-1930, as in The
> Lutheran Book of Worship)

> Lord, dismiss us with your blessing,
> fill our hearts with joy and peace.
> Let us each, your love possessing,
> triumph in redeeming grace.
> Oh, refresh us, oh, refresh us,
> travelling through this wilderness.
> (Text by John Fawcett,
> 1740-1817, as in The
> Lutheran Book of Worship)

In the Jewish tradition renewal is associated with creation itself. Shabbat is considered a momentary return to creation that causes re-creation in the lives of those who observe it. That is why one inaugurates shabbat by celebrating that theme. Though the ritual varies from one household to another, the mother's lighting of the candles to betoken God's first act in creation, the calling forth of light, and the father's recitation of the liturgy that is the opening chapter of the Torah reaffirm creation for the sake of what that will do in the lives of those who so affirm it. As the stately lines about the six days of creation are recited up to the climactic announcement of the seventh, the day of rest, the celebrants are assured that God's world is in order and has been sustained for another week by divine mercy. Life can go on. Each person at the table is renewed for the experience of yet another week.

To hallow the seventh day is to get in touch with creation itself. It is to take a step out of the world of clocks and schedules into a world of natural rhythms. Just as the sun gives us our sense of a year, so the moon gives us months that divide into the familiar quarters we call weeks. Shabbat celebrates that primeval rhythm. It is a pause that refreshes by putting us back in step with creative origins. The very day is a gift of creation and hence, of the Creator. It is grace in the form of time.

Abraham Heschel, to whom we shall pay more attention in a later chapter, has understood this aspect of shabbat especially well. In one of his best works, GOD IN SEARCH OF MAN, we find these succinct lines.

> By our acts of labor during the six days we participate in the works of history; by sanctifying the day we are reminded of those acts that surpass, ennoble and redeem history.
>
> Civilization is on trial. Its future will depend upon how much of the Sabbath will penetrate its spirit.[4]

In Heschel's understanding, actual renewal takes place with the keeping of shabbat. And that renewal goes beyond the renewal of the individuals who participate. To Heschel it was an essential renewal of history itself. Heschel could say that Sabbath renews history in the way that many a Christian will say that Christ does it. By means of two different symbols the Jew and the Christian assert the same reality.

It is not true, of course, that most Jewish people experience the grace of shabbat in any conscious way. That experience seems real only to those who care to devote themselves to it.

I recall a certain Sabbath when I was with Jewish friends in the city of Jerusalem. My friends were Americans who did not in any observable way do anything to observe it. Unless there was a private observation that I failed to notice, they treated it as a day like any other day of the week. Somewhat disappointed by this, I walked over to Me'a She'arim, where Hasidic and Orthodox Jewish people reside. There I saw the full effect of shabbat. The quarter was transformed. The somberness of everyday male garb had given way to shiny black, sparkling white and handsome hats. The women and girls had blossomed with the colors of the rainbow. The streets were closed to business and had become avenues of religious procession as happy families walked to *schul*. Life had been transformed by the mere occurrence of the Sabbath Day. The day was a day full of Grace.

Shabbat as a special time of grace is romantically explained by Hillel Seidman in his volume, THE GLORY OF THE JEWISH HOLIDAYS, by such concise statements as the following.

> On the Sabbath the Jew finds himself on an island of peace, away from the surging burdens of daily toil. On this day he dwells in a sacred palace, in the House of God --a title which is not the monopoly of the synagogue but which every truly Jewish home can attain. What the Temple is in space, the Sabbath is in time.

> The common notion is that on the Sabbath the Jew is isolated from the world. This may be so. But what is overlooked is that the Sabbath fashions a new world for him. True, so far as he is concerned, all worldly activity ceases, and he lifts himself beyond the world in its affairs --but he does not become suspended in a vacuum. On the Sabbath he lives a life which, albeit of distinct dimension and different values, is rich in content and in purpose.[5]

Seidman goes on to explain a tradition that is found in many sources, namely, that on shabbat the Jew is given "an additional soul" (*neshamah yethera*). There is the suggestion that this is the truer self that will emerge in full manifestation when the messianic age has arrived or we have been transported to a world better than this. As one reflects upon that one realizes that such are the aspirations or claimed experiences of persons in other religious traditions as well. Indeed, the very point of being religious seems to be for the sake of periodic renewal or such kind of transformation.

The idea that God desires pleasure and joy for us is a peculiarly Jewish understanding of divine grace. Shabbat is the prime occasion and, consequently, shabbat has become the very symbol of the joy provided by God. Shabbat is to be enjoyed. Therefore one lights candles, drinks wine, eats fine foods, dresses in the best of clean garments and even wears jewelry. The aura of shabbat is the aura of a holiday. There are traditional shabbat laws that are not laws at all, but what some Christians might call gospel permissions. In Millgram's book from which we already cited, there are traditional admonitions for the preparation of choice meats and the purchase of the finest wines one can afford for the occasion, the setting of the table with the finest white cloth. The preparations are to be as the preparations for a distinguished guest. The bread

to be broken must be special bread (often braided *hallah* of white flour only).
If possible, the family must dine well and in style. From the opening meal to
the closing service (havdalah), all should celebrate.

I recall some summers in Moshav Meron, a settlement of Orthodox Jews
in the Upper Galilee, where shabbat was quite properly kept by the entire
community. There were the ritual baths, first for the women and girls, then for
the men and boys. Then there were the laying out of tables in each home and
the walk to the beth knesset. Everyone who appeared in the streets was
scrubbed and well dressed, not only for the eve that was the beginning of the
occasion but throughout the full day that followed. On the Sabbath day itself
there was leisurely walking and talking, a community picnic of cold foods
prepared the day before, some frolicking on the part of the young and general
relaxation for the old. It seemed dominantly to be a day of permission, a day
when no work and little effort were required. Shabbat was a day of recreation
in the original sense of that word.

The parting ritual for shabbat, which is called the service of havdalah,
accentuates the joy of the occasion. The head of the household or one who
plays that role for a larger group, recited benedictions over wine, spices and a
lighted candle that is held by a child. One of the prayers used by some is this.

> Behold, God is my salvation. I will trust and will not
> be afraid, for the Lord is my strength and my song.
> He is become my salvation. Therefore with joy shall
> ye draw waters out of the wells of salvation.
> Salvation belongeth unto the Lord: thy blessing be
> upon thy people. The Lord of hosts is with us; the
> God of Jacob is our refuge. I will lift the cup of
> salvation and call upon the name of the Lord.[6]

There are blessings over the wine, the spices and the candle, then
perhaps songs and dancing. As shabbat was welcomed, so shabbat departs in a
spirit of joy. Her presence was God's grace in the midst of human community.

At this point the Christian reader may be puzzling and saying something
like this: wait a minute; I don't like this definition of grace. Somehow it seems
sort of loose and imprecise.

Each thoughtful Christian person is likely to have his or her own precise
definition of the term which, to be sure, compounds the problem of
communication. Therefore I must now advise the reader that precise definitions

will have to give way to broader definitions. If that does not happen, nothing else will happen by way of communication between Christians and Jews. One must realize that words are only words and that different people can be speaking of a common reality with remarkably different words. Here we are trying to get at a certain reality that Christians refer to when they use the word *grace*. The word is a Christian word. Jewish people do not commonly use the word. That does not mean that they know nothing of the reality to which the word refers. It only means that they use different terms to express it.

It may also be said that "language" includes more than the words we use. In the realm of religion it includes various symbols, including those that are ritualistic in nature. While the reality comes to the Christian as "grace" and through such channels as the blessed sacraments or the preaching of the Word, the same reality is known to Jews in other terms.

In this chapter I have asserted that the experience of shabbat (Sabbath) can be an experience of divine grace to Jewish people. Not that it necessarily is, for most Jewish people of our time seem to neglect it. Only that it is for some people and can be for others.

I have also asserted that the nature of this grace is described by using such words as renewal, freedom or recreation, that persons who experience shabbat as a graceful reality experience something that can be described by such words as freedom or renewal. To communicate that to my fellow Christians I can remind them the importance of the phrase "free gift" in Christian vocabulary. Protestant Christians in particular like to refer to grace as God's free gift.

Now shabbat is very much considered a "free gift" by those Jews who appreciate it. It is a free gift of creation. It is built into the very order of the earth. It is part of the natural time cycle and, as such, it is from God. The seventh day is the mark of the quarter moon. That is why the Torah ties it to creation and, in Exodus 20, asserts that it is a holy day because God made it holy from the beginning. The gift of Sabbath was established before any of us were born into the world. As with all gifts of grace, it awaits us with no conditions attached. We need not earn the right to receive it. It is a truly free gift that offers itself for whenever a person will take it.

In the Book of Deuteronomy a second reason is given for shabbat that makes it fully as much a matter of grace as the first. As the reason for shabbat is given in Deut. 6:12-15, we see that the Sabbath was truly made for man and not man for the Sabbath. It is for the benefit of weary creatures that God made shabbat, according to this source. All who work, be they masters, slaves or beasts of burden, need it for the sake of rejuvenation. Shabbat is given as an act of divine concern. It is for our welfare that shabbat was ordained. God sees our need for rest and revitalization. Therefore He provides this privilege of ceasing from labor, this escape and freedom from the bondage of our own rhythms of work and organization. That privilege, that freedom, is grace. There is no better word for it in Christian vocabulary.

In the spirit of this reality and our discussion of it, I would now like to offer a hymn which I composed for use in Jewish synagogues and homes. I offer it as a Christian who has come to appreciate it through sharing and experience. The thought behind the offering, I suppose, is this: that one does not have to be Jewish to experience and appreciate things that are Jewish.

> Amazing, most amazing, is the light
> that shines from star to star
> and beams upon this planet from afar,
> giving vision to our mortal eyes
> that we may see the glory of creation
> and rejoice because we are alive this day.
>
> Amazing, most amazing, are the seas
> whose breakers beat the sand
> and swelling tides that circle every land,
> producing mist and clouds of rain
> that we might hear the thunder of creation
> and rejoice because we are alive this day.
>
> Amazing, most amazing, is the earth
> whose mighty mountains rise
> above the seas and clouds to meet the skies,
> stretching fields before our mortal feet
> that we may walk in praise of all creation
> and rejoice because we are alive this day.
>
> Amazing, most amazing, are the spheres
> that whirl in endless space
> in rhythms that give sense of time and place,
> making days and years for mortal life
> that we may know the order of creation
> and rejoice because we are alive this day.

14

Amazing, most amazing, is the life
that fills the teeming sea
and flits about the earth from tree to tree,
producing sound and song for mortal ears
that we may know the wonder of creation
and rejoice because we are alive this day.

Amazing, most amazing, is the breath
that fills the fragile frames
of beasts and men whose substance is the same,
giving oneness to our mortal lives
that we may live in peace with all creation
and rejoice because we are alive this day.

Amazing, most amazing is the promise
that the Lord of all creation
has commanded Sabbath rest and celebration,
granting health for mortal spirit
that we may sing the glory of our Maker
and rejoice because we are alive this day.

In composing this offering of words, I began with the lead words in the Christian folk hymn, "Amazing Grace." From there I moved to the great liturgy of creation and Sabbath, the opening chapter of the Torah. It permitted me to join my Christian heritage with something I love of Judaism. I wrote this in the hope that such blending is both possible and desirable.

THE GRACE OF FORGIVENESS

At least a few Christians will insist that God's grace and the forgiveness of sins must go together, that forgiveness is the heart and center of it. In fact, it may well be that to some Christian people the matters of divine grace and forgiveness are so closely associated that there is no other form of divine grace than the forgiveness of sins. Guilt and forgiveness are so central to the religion of many Christian people that grace itself can be limited to that aspect of religious experience.

For those same Christian people it seems that there is no experience of divine forgiveness outside the Christian formula for it. Apart from Christ, no forgiveness: that is how stringently and simply it is understood. And failing to see the Christ formula at work in the Jewish tradition, they assume that Jewish people know nothing of God's forgiveness in their lives.

In reality, nothing could be farther from the truth. Jewish people and their Israelite forebearers knew much of God's forgiveness long before the appearance of Jesus in history. One need only browse through the ancient Book of Psalms to find the world's most eloquent statements of that experience. Even Christians appeal commonly to Psalms 32 and 51 to articulate their faith in God's forgiveness. And whether one explores the narrative or the hortatory sections of the Old Testament one will find the theme. The story of King David is a convincing demonstration of it in narrative material. Isaiah 40-55 is an extraordinarily powerful prophetic proclamation of it. In short, from the beginning of Judaic tradition the reality of God's forgiveness is recognized from the very beginning that is the foundation of Christian scripture.

Nor is it only in the Bible that we find it. We will be able to show that Jewish people have been experiencing and writing of God's forgiveness ever since Biblical times. It is an important facet of the Jewish religious experience.

For devout Jewish people, forgiveness is an especially profound experience in the season known as the High Holy Days.

The season begins with Rosh Hashanah, "head of the year," which takes place in late September or early October on the common calendar. There is a dual theme to Rosh Hashanah: the renewal of the earth and the judgment of the Almighty. The theme of judgment extends through the next ten day period which is known as the Days of Awe. The end and culmination of it all is Yom Kippur, the Day of Atonement.

As the season begins, even those who casually keep it send new year's greetings to their friends. "May you be inscribed for a good year" is a typical text. The idea behind it is that God alone can turn one year to the next and that God alone knows who is destined to live or to die in the year to come, what is destined to end and what is destined to continue.

The total season is regarded as a time of new beginnings, of renewal. But new beginnings call for corrections or purifications of what was not good in the old. If renewal is to take place, it must be prefaced by judgment. Therefore the judgment of God is a dominant theme throughout the season.

Some prayers typical to the occasion illustrate the dual theme of judgment yet hope for renewal.

> Blessed are You, for You form light and darkness, You create peace and all things. Blessed are You, for in love You chose Israel for your service.

> Our Father, our King, we have sinned before You. Inscribe us in the book of happy life, inscribe us in the book of redemption and salvation, inscribe us in the book of sustenance, inscribe us in the book of merit for a meritorious life, inscribe us in the book of forgiveness and pardon.

> Here I am, poor in good deeds, appearing with trembling awe before Him who listens to the praises of Israel. I have come to plead on behalf of your people who have sent me. Though I have not the moral purity to perform so sacred a task, I crave your peace and favor. Receive my supplications as You would those uttered by one who is fully deserving.

> May my congregation not suffer because of my sins
> and shortcomings and may the discipline of these holy
> days bring us all joy, peace and spiritual truth.
> Blessed are You who listens to our prayers.[1]

Rosh Hashanah is an announcement of what is to take place. The Days of Awe which follow are to be days when one ponders the judgment of the Almighty and does what one can to prepare for that in one's life. To illustrate the importance of that there is deliberate attention paid to a story in the Torah known as the *akedah*, the Binding of Isaac, Like the father and son in that story, every Jew is to submit him or herself completely to the will of God. God's judgment includes God's total right to impose upon us whatever his will might be. Yet from the beginning and throughout there is an expression of hope for those realities that anyone would have to call the gifts of God's grace.

One must, of course, be ready for the reception of those gifts, especially for the gift of forgiveness. In Judaism as in all religions, there is no experience of sin's forgiveness without prior repentance or penance. For the purpose of accomplishing that, the tradition has set aside the Days of Awe. The idea is that in those days one must ponder the past, honestly own up to all failures and misdeeds, undo what can be undone, pay any damages that can be paid, make apologies where apologies are needed and, after that, after doing all that one can do on one's own, one can approach the throne of The Judge and ask for divine forgiveness.

One is reminded of the remarks that Jesus of Nazareth made concerning this as they are recorded by the evangelist Matthew. In Matt. 6:23-24 we read this.

> If, when offering your gift at the altar, you remember
> that your brother has any grievance against you, leave
> your gift at the altar and go. First be reconciled to
> your brother, then come back and offer your gift.

The Holy High Days of Judaism put this advice into practice. One cannot go first to God when one has sinned against a neighbor. One must first go to the neighbor and work out forgiveness there. Once again it is as Jesus put it. One cannot experience the forgiveness of God unless one practices forgiveness with one's neighbor. "Forgive as we forgive" is a very Jewish prayer.

No matter how intense or thorough the process of repentance must be, the prayers of the season indicate an expectation of divine forgiveness as the inevitable outcome of it. On Rosh Hashanah itself, prior to the beginning of the process, the Jew may say, "He shows mercy and has compassion on his handiwork. He clothes Himself in charity. He forgives the people who are chastened in His judgment and purifies those who trust him."

Underlying all that is to be done in the Days of Awe and on Yom Kippur is the concept of *teshuvah*. *Teshuvah*, which literally means "returning," is the Hebrew word that is often translated as repentance. The significance of it is that one experiences renewal as one returns to God, to the Source of our being. Because God demands goodness, the return involves judgment and possible correction. Yet it necessarily eventuates in forgiveness. The judgment and the forgiveness go together. There is not one aspect without the other. The whole formula is *turn and be saved*. There is no such thing as repentance without the forgiveness, as judgment without mercy. The grace is part of the formula. This means that "repent" cannot be a threatening word, at least as Judaism understands it. It is, in fact, a word of promise. Because repentance leads to forgiveness, it is a positive and encouraging experience. Judaism is disposed to understand the positive conclusion of Jesus' concise statement as recorded in Mark 1:16, which reads, "The Kingdom of God is at hand; *repent and believe in the good news.*" The repentance that is encouraged by Jewish tradition is repentance in the context of grace.

The culmination of the High Holy Days is the Yom Kippur service itself. There the confession of sin is intensified and forgiveness is daringly requested. In a part of the service a participant may read this list of the attributes of God's mercy as based on Exodus 34.

(1) God is merciful to one who has the intention and is about to sin. Even as the sinful act is contemplated, God's mercy continues to function as a deterrent.

(2) God is forgiving to the sinner who has repented.

(3) God is powerful to act as His wisdom dictates. In his wisdom he has granted man moral freedom to choose between right and wrong without losing any part of His all-powerfulness.

(4) God is gracious to those who have fallen, and assists them to rise.

(5) God is patient and ever hopeful that the sinner will repent.

(6) God is generous both to the righteous and the wicked.

(7) God is truthful and faithful to carry out his promises.

(8) God performs acts of loving-kindness to thousands and gives them credit for the merit of their fathers.

(9) God forgives sins committed even with premeditation.

(10) God forgives sins committed in the spirit of rebellion against Him.

(11) God forgives sins committed inadvertently.

(12) God not only forgives but "wipes the slate clean."[2]

Such statements as those just recited are the convictions of a people who truly believe in the grace of God. Forgiveness is expected. Not without the preparation of repentance, to be sure, but with the assumption that the gracious forgiveness is there and waiting. Just as surely as a Christian may go to the altar of the Lord's Supper with the expectation of mercy, so may a Jew go to the service of Yom Kippur. Forgiveness really does happen for the one who does it. It is expected and it takes place.

There is a folk custom kept by many as part of the total ritual of the season that takes the worshippers to the side of a river, stream, pond or lake to act out the words of Micah 7:19, "You will drown all our sins deep in the sea." An especially charming account of it is given us by Bella Chagall in her autobiographical writings that now appear in the volume, FIRST ENCOUNTERS (pp. 51-52).[3]

> I could hardly wait for the afternoon, when I would go with Mother to the Tashlich ceremony to cast my sins in the river.
>
> On the way we met other men and women, all going through the narrow street down to the river bank. They were all dressed in black, as if they were going, God forbid, to a funeral. The air was cool; a crisp breeze was blowing from the public gardens on the steep river bank. Red and yellow leaves fell from the trees, flitting like butterflies, twirling around us, then falling to the ground. Did our sins fly away from us in the same way?

The leaves rustled and stuck to our shoes. I tried to make them cling on, to make the Tashlich seem less frightening.

"What are you dawdling for? Let the leaves alone," said Mother, dragging me along.

Soon everyone came to a halt. The street seemed to break off. The deep, cold water lapped at our feet. Dark-clad groups of people were gathered on the bank. Bearded men leaned over the water as if they wanted to see right to the bottom.

Suddenly they turned out their pockets, and crumbs and bits of fluff fell out of the linings. They prayed aloud, casting their sins into the water at the same time as the crumbs.

But how was I going to cast away my sins? I had no crumbs in my pockets. I didn't even have any pockets.

I stood at Mother's side, shivering in the cold wind that blew up our skirts.

She whispered the ritual words to me, and my sins fell with the prayers out of my mouth into the water. It seemed to me the river swelled with our sins, that its waters suddenly turned black.

Home I went, purified.

In a great book by S. Y. Agnon titled DAYS OF AWE, there is an especially beautiful account of the joy of forgiveness as experienced by some Jewish people at Yom Kippur. We quote from pages 276-7.[4]

Let every man set his table and eat joyfully and with a good heart, as on a night when a holiday is hallowed, for on this day all his transgressions are forgiven, the mercy of the Lord being with him. The same is written in the Midrash: "At the close of Yom Kippur a voice issues from heaven and says, `Go thy way, eat thy bread with joy, and drink thy wine with a merry heart; for God hath already accepted thy works' (Eccles. 9:7); and your prayer has been heard" (Eccles. Rabbah III). The masters of the Tosafot (Shabbat 114), also, wrote that the close of Yom Kippur is a kind of holiday.

Yom Kippur itself can be a dramatic and moving experience that is made all the more effective when skilled singers can perform the powerful texts and music that tradition provides. It may well be that for many Jewish people the sheer beauty and drama of the occasion are the sum of its appeal. As is the case with Christians who attend worship at Christmas and Easter because of beauty and quality of those occasions, so also in the Jewish tradition there is respect for that which is artistic and done well. Yet there are also those people who value it because of what happens. Through the vehicle of music, words and presentation a person can experience catharsis and renewal. The event can be a truly internal event that renews, uplifts, strengthens or changes a human life. The event can be a truly internal event that renews, uplifts, strengthens or changes a human life. The event can be as a gift, as an experience of grace.

As one compares one religion with another it is wise to compare one feature to another on the basis of what is truly experienced by the participants. This means that superficial similarities may not be very important.

Because Jews and Christians celebrate Passover and Easter at approximately the same time, we tend to compare those two occasions. Nowadays many a Christian congregation even celebrates a semblance of Passover on the Thursday evening of Holy week --realizing that some such celebration was the origin of the Christian Eucharist. There is always something uncomfortable about that, of course. While the seder service of Pessah is a truly happy occasion, the Maundy Thursday commemoration is a solemn one that looks toward the tragic story of Good Friday. The quality of Passover and the quality of Christians Holy Week are clearly not the same.

If I were to name the Christian holiday that is most like Passover in what actually happens for the people who participate, I would name Christmas as a parallel. At both Christmas and Passover there is a happy gathering of families and feasting that celebrates that gathering. In addition to that, both occasions celebrate important beginnings. For Jews, Passover celebrates the birth of the nation in the story of the Exodus. For Christians, Christmas celebrates the birth of the Child who is very much the beginning point for Christianity.

As for a parallel to the Jewish High Holy Days, what better compares to it than Christian Lent and Holy Week? Traditionally, it is Lent and Holy Week that permit the Christian to ponder the mysteries of guilt, confession and forgiveness. Lent leads into the sad and sombre time of their Lord's crucifixion and Easter resolves it with the announcement of resurrection and renewed life. A Christian can experience the renewal of forgiveness in a special way in the season that culminates with Easter. A Jew experiences the same in the days that culminate with Yom Kippur. In both of these holy seasons what is celebrated is the grace of divine forgiveness.

THE GRACE OF SACRED SEASONS

It may be somewhat true to say that sacred holidays are times of grace in any religious tradition. Not that they necessarily function that way for everyone in the tradition but that they are available for that realization to those who make use of them in a meaningful way.

Each of the Jewish festivals is, in one way or another, a reminder of the grace of God. "By divine grace we endure" could well be the motto of the sum total of them all. The old nature festivals, Succot and Shavuot and the early Feast of Unleavened Bread, were reminders of God's sustenance through nature's annual gifts. Hannukah and Purim both celebrate survival in the face of hostile odds. Even Tish'ah B'av and Shoah celebrate survival in a reverse fashion, for both of those commemorations testify that the Jewish people live on despite all disasters.

Pessah is particularly rich with images and expressions of divine grace. The prayers that punctuate the seder service all testify to God's grace as the Giver of gifts.

> Blessed are You, Lord our God, Ruler of the universe,
>
> Creator of the fruit of the vine.
> ...., Creator of light and fire.
>
> ...., who has given us life and sustenance and brought us to this happy season.
>
> ...., Creator of the fruit of the earth.
>
> ...., who sustains the whole universe in his good-ness, with grace, loving-kindness and mercy. He gives food to all, for his mercy endures forever. In

> his great goodness he never failed us with sustenance
> and may he never fail us, for the sake of his great
> name. It is he who provides for all, sustains all and
> is beneficent to all, preparing food for all his
> creatures whom he created. Blessed are you, O Lord,
> who provides food for all.
>
> ...., for the vine and for the fruit of the vine, for
> the produce of the field and for that precious, good
> and spacious land which You gave to our ancestors,
> to eat of its fruit and to enjoy its goodness.
>
> ...., Creator of innumerable living beings. We
> thank You for all the means that You have created to
> sustain all.[1]

The special focus of the festival is, of course, Israel's redemption out of
Egypt by the grace of God alone. Whether in the convenental language of
Exodus 19:1-6 or the portions of Haggadah that recite the marvelous story, the
emphasis is the same: it was a miracle of God's doing that brought Israel out of
slavery in Egypt.

The beginning of the answer to the famous Four Questxpions sets the
emphasis clearly.

> We were slaves of Pharaoh in Egypt and the Lord our
> God brought us out from there with a strong hand and
> an outstretched arm. Now if God had not brought
> our forefathers out of Egypt, then even we might still
> be enslaved. Therefore, even were we all wise, all
> men of understanding, even if we were all old and
> well learned in the Torah, it would still be our duty to
> tell the story of the departure from Egypt.

Little Christians are taught to sing, "I love to tell the story of Jesus and
his love." Young Jews learn to love another story with equally strong emphasis
on God's gracious redemption. The story of Exodus is a story of how God
decided, God acted, God redeemed with no prior proof of the merit or goodness
of the people who benefited from this.

One of the popular songs of Pessah emphasizes the idea that Israel was/is
beholden to God every step of the way. Whether God had done little or much,
one must acknowledge gratitude and dependence on the unilateral deed of
redemption. The song "*dayyenu*" begins like this.

> How thankful must we be to God, the All-Present,
> for all the good He did for us.
> Had He brought us out from Egypt

> and not executed judgment against them,
> it would have been enough for us.
> Had He executed judgment against them
> and not done justice to their idols,
> it would have been enough for us.
> Had He done justice to their idols
> and not slain their firstborn,
> it would have been enough for us.
> Etc.

The entire story is recited in this manner, emphasizing with the refrain, "it would have been enough for us," that every step of the way, that each part of the event was a gift of divine grace.

At the point of the second cup of wine the prayers emphasize this very strongly.

> Therefore it is our duty to thank and praise in song and prayer, to glorify and extol Him who performed all these wonders for our forefathers and for us. He brought us out of slavery to freedom, from anguish to joy, from sorrow to festivity, from darkness to great light. Let us therefore sing before Him a new song. Praise the Eternal.

> Blessed are You, Lord our God, Ruler of the universe, who redeemed us and redeemed our forefathers from Egypt and brought us to this night to eat there on matzah and bitter herbs. Thus may the Lord our God and God of our fathers bring us to future feasts and festivals in peace, and to the upbuilding of your city Jerusalem and to the happiness of your service, so that we may partake there of the ancient offerings and then offer unto You a new song for our redemption and salvation. Blessed are You, Lord, who redeemed Israel.

As the prayers indicate, the celebration of redemption out of Egypt in ancient times becomes the celebration of God's continuing redemption of Israel and all future redemption as well. Therefore, and in anticipation of ultimate redemption, the feast ends with the cry, "Next year in Jerusalem!" The alpha of the ancient birth of the nation is merged with the omega of final redemption.

Redemption is the key word in the celebration. While to Christians *salvation* is more commonly the key word that connects to the idea of the grace of God, for Jewish people it is the concept of redemption. What is the meaning of this term?

Within Hebrew tradition, redemption is complementary to creation. What was once created by the Creator will also be redeemed by the Creator when redemption is necessary. To redeem is to reclaim, to seek and to save what is lost, to liberate what is in bondage. To redeem a slave, one ransoms that slave from bondage. To redeem a sick or wounded person, one heals and brings back to wholeness. To redeem a destitute family is to provide for that family and reinstate its status of honor among other families. To redeem is to reclaim the value of something or someone whose value has been lost or not seen for some time.

Jews typically see themselves as a people who have been repeatedly redeemed by God's mercy. The Exodus, which was redemption from bondage in Egypt, is taken as the initial and primary example of that. Therefore *Pessah* is a festival of redemption. And most of the other festivals continue that theme, for, as we noted before, most Jewish festivals celebrate survival and to celebrate survival is to celebrate redemption.

Looking to their past, Jewish people see themselves as a people who took their place among the peoples of the earth because God, the Lord of history, redeemed them out of Egypt, out of Babylon and out of nearly innumerable diaspora situations. Recalling the centuries from the ancient Exodus to now, they feel themselves to be a people repeatedly redeemed from disaster and annihilation. As Passover is celebrated they express the hope that redemption will continue, that they may live on and "see Jerusalem."

Some episodes in history call this into question, most particularly the disastrous events of World War II. Indeed, that holocaust has moved many Jews away from traditional faith. In the place of faith in God's grace they have put their faith in their own guts and determination. Yet it has not killed the faith of the total Jewish community. There are still those to whom *Pessah* and other sacred festivals are powerful reminders of the grace of the Almighty. The fact that again and again "a remnant" is redeemed seems some sort of proof of it. And even to those who claim not to be religious, the survival of Israel seems some sort of mystery if not a miracle.

Among liberal Jews who are religious, particularly in the Reform movement, the concept of redemption is extended to include the whole world. For at least some of them, *Pessah* can be a celebration of earth's repeated redemption. A good example of this kind of thinking is to be seen in the following excerpt from Kaufman Kohler's book, JEWISH THEOLOGY.

> However burdensome the Passover minutiae, especially in regard to the prohibition of leaven, became to the Jewish household, the predominant feature was always an exuberance of joy. In the darkest days of medievalism the synagogue resounded with song and thanksgiving, and the young imbibed the joy and comfort of their elders through the beautiful symbols of the feast and the richly adorned tale of the deliverance. The Passover feast with its "night of divine watching" endowed the Jew ever anew with endurance during the dark night of medieval tyranny and with faith in "the Keeper of Israel who slumbereth not nor sleepeth." Moreover, as the spring-tide of nature fills each creature with joy and hope, so Israel's feast of redemption promises the great day of liberty to those who still chafe under the yoke of oppression. The modern Jew is beginning to see in the reawakening of his religious and social life in western lands the token of the future liberation of all mankind. The Passover feast brings him the clear and hopeful message of freedom for humanity from all bondage of body and spirit.[2]

Judaism has various symbols of redemption, which is to say various symbols of this aspect of divine grace. In the *Pessah* service we recognize such symbols as the Exodus, Moses, the foods (especially those that signal springtime), and Jerusalem. In addition to these there is the colorful figure of the prophet Elijah. In a spirit of fun as well as some measure of devotion, there is attention to the possible arrival of this figure at each annual celebration. At the table there is a special place set for Elijah and a special cup of wine poured for his appearing. Near the close of the seder service the door is opened and he may be welcomed by the singing of the folksy "Eliyahu Hanavee" (Elijah the Prophet). Stories abound as to how in one secret way or another he does appear and in almost ever case his visit is a visit of salvation in which the assemble guests are spared from one disaster or another. it seems that Elijah wanders the earth in the interest of preserving God's people while he waits for the day when he can announce the appearing of the Messiah. The tales of Elijah are tales of God's preserving grace.

The legendary or mythical figure of Elijah provides one more point of contact for Christians and Jews, for he is a figure common to both traditions. A Christian must remember that John, the baptizing prophet of the Jordan and contemporary of Jesus, has been given the name of Elijah in the earliest Christian records, those of the New Testament itself. As the announcer of the Age of Redemption, Elijah is himself a symbol of it. To welcome his appearance is to anticipate and desire the transformation that God's grace can accomplish in human history. And whether Elijah be the historical (and legendary) figure of John or the colorfully legendary figure of Jewish tradition, the figure is in both cases a symbol of divine redemption.

The concept of redemption is a concept that Christians can do well to ponder insofar as it functions as a near synonym to the term *grace*. It is, to be sure, a word more common and precious to the Jewish than to the Christian tradition. Yet it is not a strange word to Christians and can be an important word as well. For one thing, it is a word that can be used to speak of the career of Jesus. It can be truthfully said that the work of Jesus was the work of redemption and that his announcement of The Kingdom was an announcement of God's redemption.

It was the evangelist Luke who particularly emphasized the redemptive aspect of Jesus' ministry, for it was Luke who loved to portray him as that one who came to seek and to save the lost. As we follow Jesus through that gospel record, we follow a man who had a special eye for those who needed redemption in one way or another --the sick, the disowned, the disrespected, the disadvantaged. As Luke portrayed him, he was a man who came to liberate, to heal, to declare worthy. What God does for Israel through history is what Jesus is pictured as doing for the least of those who were Israelites in his day and, to lift a line from another gospel writing, for the least of all his brethren.

Redemption is a fitting word for what Christians call the grace of God. So when Jewish people celebrate that, they are celebrating divine grace.

For both Jews and Christians there is a psalm which does a good job of articulating what redemption is all about. It is the Bible's Psalm 107.

> "praise the lord, for he is good;
>   his steadfast love is eternal!"
> thus let the redeemed of the lord say,

those he redeemed from adversity,
whom he gathered in from the lands,
from east and west,
from the north and from the sea.

some lost their way in the wilderness,
in the wasteland;
they found no settled place.
hungry and thirsty,
their spirit failed.
in their adversity they cried to the lord,
and he rescued them from their troubles.
he showed them a direct way
to reach a settled place.
let them praise the lord for his steadfast love,
his wondrous deeds for mankind;
for he has satisfied the thirsty,
filled the hungry with all good things.

some lived in deepest darkness,
bound in cruel irons,
because they defied the word of god,
spurned the counsel of the most high.
he humbled their hearts through suffering;
they stumbled with no one to help.
in their adversity they cried to the lord,
and he rescued them from their troubles.
he brought them out of deepest darkness,
broke their bonds asunder.
let them praise the lord for his steadfast love,
his wondrous deeds for mankind,
for shattered gates of bronze,
he broke their iron bars.

there were fools who suffered for their sinful way,
and for their iniquities.
all food was loathsome to them;
they reached the gates of death.
in their adversity they cried to the lord
and he saved them from their troubles.
he gave an order and healed them;
he delivered them from the pits.
let them praise the lord for his steadfast love,
his wondrous deeds for mankind.
let them offer thanksgiving sacrifices,
and tell his deeds in joyful song.

others go down to the sea in ships,
ply their trade in the mighty waters;
they have seen the works of the lord
and his wonders in the deep.
by his word he raised a storm wind
that made the waves surge.

mounting up to the heaven,
   plunging down to the depths,
   disgorging in their misery,
   they reeled and staggered like a drunken man,
   all their skill to no avail.
in their adversity they cried to the lord,
   and he saved them from their troubles.
he reduced the storm to a whisper;
   the waves were stilled.
they rejoiced when all was quiet,
   and he brought them to the port they desired.
let them praise the lord for his steadfast love,
   his wondrous deeds for mankind.
let them exalt him in the congregation of the people,
   acclaim him in the assembly of the elders.

he turns the rivers into a wilderness,
   springs of water into a thirsty land,
   fruitful land into a salt marsh,
   because of the wickedness of its inhabitants.
he turns the wilderness into pools,
   parched land into springs of water.
there he settles the hungry;
   they build a place to settle in.
they sow fields and plant vineyards
   that yield a fruitful harvest.
he blesses them and they increase greatly;
   and he does not let their cattle decrease,
   after they had been few and crushed
   by oppression, misery, and sorrow.
he pours contempt on great men
   and makes them lose their way in trackless deserts;
   but the needy he secures from suffering,
   and increases their families like flocks.

the upright see it and rejoice;
   the mouth of all wrongdoers is stopped.
the wise man will take note of these things;
   he will consider the steadfast love of the Lord.[3]

THE GRACE OF TORAH

It may be difficult for a Christian to even contemplate the notion expressed by the phrase, "the grace of Torah." Especially if the person be a Protestant Christian who has been brought up trained to think of Torah as "law" and as something quite opposite to "grace" or "gospel." And even if that not be the case, Torah is so strictly a Jewish phenomenon that only a person who has been brought up to be familiar and friendly with the term can appreciate the phrase. I am quite sure that appreciation is not even possible for most of the Jews whom I know as friends. As they tell me of themselves and their growing, they indicate either an indifferent or negative attitude toward Torah. It is a word that suggests outmoded rules and traditions. It is a word to be held dear by the orthodox alone. Only people who wear black and white and put on *tefillin* to pray can truly resonate to such a phase as "the grace of Torah."

Yet it may be that one does not have to be that narrowly or strictly traditional to know something of that grace. Any visitor who first observes Jewish worshippers touching the Torah scroll as it is paraded through the aisles on a shabbat eve or morning will come away with some impression of the veneration felt and shown toward the Torah. It is, after all, a token of God's presence. It is an embodiment of the *shekinah*. What Jesus can be or what Jesus and Mary together can be to pious Christians, the Torah scrolls can be for Jews. To touch them is to come as close as one can to touching God. To hear them read, whether in Hebrew or in translation, is to hear the very will of God enunciated for human ears. The Torah is a powerful symbol of God's presence, of God's authority in human life, of God's grace.

The annual feast of *Simhat Torah*, which climaxes the season of *Sukkot*, gives expression to the joy that is felt in response to what Jewish people consider to be a divine gift. Two anecdotes will illustrate this. The first is a tale of the Baal Shem Tov as recorded by Herman Cohen in Philip Goodman's volume, *THE SUCCOTH AND SIMHAT Torah Anthology*.

> Hasidim of the Baal shem Tov were at his home celebrating Simhat Torah with song, dance, and wine. Fearing they might exhaust the supply of wine, the host's wife complained to her husband. "Tell your disciples to cease dancing and drinking, for soon no wine will be left for Kiddush and Havdalah."

> With a smile on his lips, the Baal Shem Tov replied, "You are undoubtedly correct. Tell them to stop and go home."

> The dutiful wife opened the door of the room where the Hasidim were rejoicing. When she witnessed their pervasive spiritual ecstasy, she brought them more wine.

> Later the Baal shem Tov asked his spouse if she told them to go home. She rejoined, "You should have told them yourself!"[1]

The second is part of an account by Bella Chagall, whose memoirs we have already quoted.

> Once a year we children were allowed to run wild in the synagogue. By the evening we were worn out and breathless.

> The synagogue was packed, and there were so many boys there was hardly room to keep out of their way. Even the little girls were allowed in the men's section for the "procession" of the Torah. Boys and girls together got under the older people's feet.

> The lamps seemed to shine with a new light. The ark was open, and the Scrolls of the Law in their festive covers were brought out one by one. The synagogue became a holy temple, with the men dancing as they carried the scrolls around and the children dancing with them or keeping time with their feet.[2]

To be realistic we must recognize that the expression of joy displayed at *Simhat Torah* and similar occasions will be determined in degree by the religious devotion of the person concerned and in kind by the person's age. A fun occasion will be fun to kids no matter what. Fun, after all, is a good thing for fun's sake alone. The profound joy over Torah is reserved for those who are profound in their dedication to it.

At this point let us retreat from the notion of actually celebrating Torah to some explanation of how it is that Jewish people can even think of Torah as a gift of divine grace. Certainly, if "law" is all there is to it only very unusual personalities would be able to relate to it that positively.

Torah is perhaps best translated by the word "tradition." Yet it is not a word that can necessarily be used as a replacement for "tradition." It is only certain tradition, a certain people's tradition, that can be called by that name. It is the Torah given by Moses to Israel that is true Torah. It is the Torah of the five books or scrolls that are honored with the word.

As Jewish people understand it, *Torah* consists of two contents: narrative which is called *haggadah*, and rules or directive which are known as *halachah*.

The *haggadah* sections of Torah record the beginnings of Jewish existence. For the same reason that the Exodus (which is originally recorded in the Torah) and the rituals of *Pessah* (which are first commanded in the Torah) are reminders of God's grace, so is the whole of Torah. The whole thing is a reminder to Jewish people that they owe their existence to God and of course what one owes completely to God is a matter of divine grace.

Perhaps it is important to suggest that this should be considered a matter of grace by all people, not merely by Jews. Perhaps it is important that all people consider their very existence to be a matter of divine grace. After all, if God is defined as the Creator, then it is to God alone that we owe the fact of our existence. And this should be as true for individuals as for communal or ethnic groups.

It was in recognition of this that the great Christian reformer, Martin Luther, included the following lines in his famous and important educational tract, The Small Catechism.

> I believe that God has created me and all that exists,
> that He has given and still preserves to me my body
> and all its members.....that He daily sustains me and
> provides for all my needs.....for all of which I am in
> duty bound to thank, praise, serve and obey Him.[3]

All of creation is a matter of divine grace and my personal creation and existence should be all that more dearly a matter of grace for me.

One Hebrew prophet recognized that this should be so for each and every people on earth. In Amos 9:7 we read about how God led the Ethiopians and the Philistines and the Aramaeans as surely as He led the Israelites on their historical path.

There is also another way in which Torah can be understood as a gift of divine grace and that has to do with its legal content.

In the Torah itself we find a view of human nature that pictures us as creatures of a dual nature, possessing an urge to do good (*yetzer hattov*) and an urge to do evil (*yetzer hara'*). Caught in this dilemma, if we are left to ourselves, we are apt to turn out badly, as humans did according to the Torah's well known story of the flood. We are likely as not to be overcome by our own inclination to evil, as was Cain in the Torah's story about the first fratricide. Therefore, in the light of that, we need all the help and guidance we can get. For the Jew that help and guidance are given in the Torah. The Torah is God's way of helping the good to overcome the evil within us. It is guidance and it is a gift.

Accepting this notion (and only if one accepts this notion, we may add), it is possible to see how a person can have a good attitude toward the rules of Torah. A person who sees that its principles and rules are there to help him in his own personal struggle to be a good person will see them in a positive light. They will not be restrictions. They will be possibilities for good.

As one reads the famous Ten Words (more commonly known as the Ten Commandments) in the Hebrew text of the Book of Exodus, one can notice that the negatives are stated with the Hebrew word *lo'* rather than the word *'al*. The meaning of *lo'* plus the verb is "You don't" or "You don't have to" (murder, steal, commit adultery or whatever). An active command that says, "Don't (so such-and-such) would be given with *'al*. As they are given, the Ten Commandments state possibilities of human behavior. In effect they are saying, "You don't have to be as bad a fellow as the worst you are inclined to be. There is the possibility of goodness in you. You don't have to be a criminal, even though all the world around you be caught in crime. You can follow the path, the *halachah*, laid before you in the Torah. In the Torah you see the possibility of your goodness."

This is how Torah can be encouraging rather than discouraging, liberating rather than restrictive. When I view myself as having a problem that Torah helps me to solve, then Torah or any similar kind of guidance can be taken as a good and beneficial gift.

Much of this is a matter of attitude. If a person is brought up in an environment that lays all matters of instruction down as requirements that decide his worth as a person, that person develops a negative attitude toward it. To such a person, all matters of instruction or guidance may seem to be oppressive. Only those who have been led to see the rules as ways to avoid what is bad and get hold of what is good will view them in a positive way. That is why we cannot say that the Torah is a graceful reality to all Jews. "The grace of Torah" is a phrase that *can* be meaningful to all Jews, perhaps, but is in reality meaningful only to some or perhaps a few. (A similar remark can be made about the attitudes of various Christians to the matters of their tradition.)

For those who do feel this positive attitude there is a magnificently long psalm in the Biblical collection. It is Psalm 119, a lengthy acrostic that ponders the delights of Torah in as many ways as may be possible. For those who want a less lengthy meditation of the theme, Psalm 19 will suffice. It is a psalm which links the grace of Torah to the grace of creation.[4]

> The heavens declare the glory of God,
>   the sky proclaims His handiwork.
> Day to day makes utterance,
>   night to night speaks out.
> There is no utterance,
>   there are no words,
>   whose sound goes unheard.
> Their voice carries throughout the earth,
>   their words to the end of the world.
> He placed in them a tent for the sun,
>   who is like a groom coming forth from the chamber,
>   like a hero, eager to run his course.
> His rising-place is at one end of heaven,
>   and his circuit reaches the other;
>   nothing escapes his heat.
> The teachings of the Lord is perfect,
>   renewing life;
>   the decrees of the Lord are enduring,
>   making the simple wise;
> The precepts of the Lord are just,
>   rejoicing the heart;

the instruction of the Lord is lucid,
making the eyes light up.
The fear of the lord is pure,
abiding forever;
the judgments of the Lord are true,
righteous altogether,
more desirable than gold,
than much fine gold;
sweeter than honey,
than drippings of the comb.
Your servant pays them heed;
in obeying them there is much reward.
Who can be aware of errors?
Clear me of unperceived guilt,
and from willful sins keep Your servant;
let them not dominate me;
then shall I be blameless
and clear of grave offense.
May the words of my mouth
and the prayer of my heart
be acceptable to You,
O Lord, my rock and my redeemer.

GRACE IN RABBINIC TRADITION

One of the things I aim to show is that Jewish tradition has always had an awareness of the grace of God, from the beginning to now. I have already indicated more than once that the Old Testament shows this awareness as fully as the New. I now hope to show that the theme continues in rabbinic Judaism of the time of Jesus and continues on in the sources that follow that. I begin with the Talmud.

As is wont for a Christian or anyone who is a stranger to it, I approached the Talmud with the expectation of finding it to be a compendium of theological wisdom. I was initially disappointed, of course, for the Talmud is not that kind of literature. For the most part, the Talmud is a collection of jurisprudence that comprises both apodictic and, in greater measure, casuistic law. It is a record of the great rabbis who practiced in the first five centuries of this common era, with snippets of earlier tradition such as were extracted by R. Travers Herford in 1925 for his remarkable volume entitled PIRKE AVOT, "Chapters of the Fathers."

The rabbis of the Talmud tradition were more concerned with human affairs than the affairs of heaven. To be sure, they operated with the underlying assumption that the basic laws were given by God but they were concerned with the fact that it is mortals who must practice them and practice justice with them. The deliberations recorded in the Talmud, as delightfully (or boringly) detailed as they are, record their honest efforts to attain the maximum of justice possible in human affairs. There is an understanding that ultimate judgment belongs to God --and there are no lack of indications of that along the way-- but that ultimate judgment is grounded in ultimate mercy.

38

To illustrate the truth of this I would like to begin with a number of relevant quotations from the excerpts known as Pirke Avot and from further excerpts recorded in A RABBINIC ANTHOLOGY by Montefiore and Loewe. Assuming their permission to do so, I have loosened the translations a bit for the sake of this little volume.[1]

> Antigonus of Socho received this from Simeon the Just, who used to say: Be not like servants who serve the master in order to receive a gift but be like servants who serve with no condition. Let respect for Heaven alone by upon you.

> R. Simeon said: Be careful in reciting the Shema' and in prayer. When you pray, make your prayer not only a fixed form but actual beseeching and entreaty before God. It is said (Joel 2:13): For he is gracious and merciful, long-suffering and plenteous in mercy, and repents of evil. Be not wicked in your own sight.

> (Akiva) used to say: Beloved is man in that he was created in the image. Greater love was proved to him in that he was created in the image of God, as it is said (Gen. 9:6): In the image of God he made man. Beloved are Israel in that they are called sons of God. Greater love was proved to them in that they were called sons of God, as it is said (Deut. 14:1): You are sons to the Lord your God.

> R. Haggai said in the name of R. Isaac: All need grace. Even Abraham, for whose sake grace came plenteously into the world, needed grace.

> "Through your righteousness deliver me" (Ps. 71:2), Israel says to God. "If you save us, save us not through our righteousness or good deeds but, be it today or tomorrow, deliver us through your righteousness."

> "Deal with your servant according to your hesed (grace)" (Ps. 119:24). Perhaps you have pleasure in our good works? Merit and good works we have not. Act toward us in *hesed*. "The men of old whom you redeemed, you redeemed not through their works. You acted toward them in hesed and redeemed them."

> R. Elazar quoted Ps. 62:13: Yours, O Lord, is loving-kindness (*hesed*) for you are the one who requites each man according to his work. But if the man has no *hesed* (loving-kindness), you give of your *hesed* (grace).

> There are ten words for prayer. One of them is appeal for grace. Of all the ten, Moses used only this one, as it is said, "And I appealed for grace with the Lord at the mountain (Deut. 3:23). R. Johanan said: So you may learn that man has no claim upon God, for Moses, the greatest of all the prophets, came before God only with an appeal for grace. R. Levi said: Why did Moses do so? The proverb says, "Be careful lest you be caught by your words." God said to Moses, "I will be gracious to whom I will be gracious. To him who has nothing to his account I show mercy.....to him who has nothing I am gracious."

> It was not for their works that the Israelites were delivered from Egypt, or for their father's works. It was not by their works that the sea was divided, but to make a name for God, as it says, "Dividing the waters before them to make Himself an everlasting name" (Isa. 63:12). So Moses told the Israelites, "Not through your works were you redeemed, but so that you might praise God and declare His renown among the nations."

These passages illustrate that the concept of grace is far from absent in the early rabbinic literature. They illustrate, further, that the concept was understood the same among the great rabbis as it was (and is) among Christians. We are in error when we assert that Christianity grasped and taught the grace of God while Judaism did not. There were, to be sure, those Jews who did not. But there are also Christians who do not (we may call them false Christians if we wish). The dividing line between those who have experienced it and those who have not is not a line that divides one religion from another. It is more likely a line that divides one from another within any or all religious traditions.

In the passages quoted there was reference to a Hebrew word written as *hesed*. It is an important term that lies behind the New Testament words for the grace and love of God. In its Old Testament usage the word is used to speak of behavior that is determined by a bond such as the bond between parents and their children, between siblings in a family, between lifelong friends. The Biblical writers asserted that such a bond at its strongest is the bond between the Creator and His creation.

Hesed is the kindness that is dependably there because of the commitment demanded by that bond. *Hesed* is dependable kindness. It is like compassion and allegiance combined. Early English translators of the Bible coined a word for the sake of translating it. That word was *loving-kindness*. *Hesed* is a common word in the Old Testament and a common word in the tradition of Jewish literature, be it in the original or in translation. It is an especially common word in the Biblical Psalms and in devotional literature.

Hesed can be used of human behavior but when it is so used it is to imply that human behavior should be a reflection of God's behavior --that humans should be loving toward each other as God is loving toward all his creation and that human love or kindness should be as dependable as the *hesed* of God. *Hesed* is what is often called "undeserved kindness," for it means to refer to love or favor that we don't have to earn or deserve because it is there prior to our very desire for it.

This means, of course, that when Christians talk about the "undeserved love of God" they are not the only ones to do so. Jewish people are also accustomed to that kind of talk. Jews and Christians together have inherited the concept embodied in the Hebrew word *hesed*.

Following a Jewish way of thinking, one can say that man was created in order to give opportunity for God to display his forgiveness, his loving-kindness, his mercy, his grace. God expects humans to be and to do good and ascribes merit to those who honestly display this by the lives they live. But beyond all human merit are the compassion and grace of God. God stands ready for all human shortcoming, ready to receive even the smallest indication of genuine repentance, and is never weary of listening to the cry of His human creatures in their various distresses. That is Jewish religious thinking. That is a Jewish understanding of divine grace.

The Talmudic sages obviously operated with an effective polarity of understanding which on the one hand honored God's justice and, on the other hand, recognized the necessity of grace. They saw in the laws of God the implication that goodness was possible, for the laws were meant to be kept, but they saw in human behavior the propensity to weakness if not the evil and in that they saw the necessity for grace. Their immense respect for God's authority and justice simply made their understanding of God's grace all that much more profound. It was primarily in the realm of ethics that they came to see it this way, of course. Dealing with ethical issues was the substance of their livelihood. In practicing their profession as sages and judges, they were faced with sinners who were caught in both minor and major offences and disputes. While they sought peace between contenders and rectification vis a vis the community, they were also aware of the sinner's station before the Almighty and of the quality of mercy at that Throne that transcended their own. Where their own mercy fell short, they knew that divine mercy did not. Where they had to pass judgment they knew that God might dispense forgiveness. They understood their own limits within the context of the limitlessness of divine grace.

Every great religion propends to feel that it has a near monopoly on the grace of God. To an Orthodox Jew it is unthinkable that any but the most exceptional gentile has access to it. To the fanatic Moslem there is no grace for infidels. For the Christian of such historic strains as Greek Orthodoxy, Roman Catholicism or Lutheranism, only those who are properly members of The Church (their church) are saved. For historical Christians, the proper conversion or adherence to the proper doctrines or a special gift of the Spirit are the only routes of access.

All of this seems quite presumptuous, of course. All seem to be making exclusive claims to something that seems common to all traditions. If all can speak of "unmerited grace" (in whatever terms) and if all equally stress their humble dependence on the goodness of God, there is something comic about their claims. The grace of God is surely the same wherever it operates. Perhaps our experience of it is the same as well, despite all differences of vocabulary or tradition.

IBERIAN GRACE

During the long period known to Western Christians as the Middle Ages or even as the Dark Ages, there was a great flowering of Moslem and Jewish culture in the Iberian peninsula. The flowering was broad in its scope, comprising the arts, the sciences and commerce. It also included the creative writing of a considerable amount of religious literature among the Jews. Therefore, to follow the theme of grace in Jewish tradition beyond the period of the Talmud, we shall now turn to the works of the Jewish poets of Spain.

As one reads over the various works of some dozen well known Jewish poets of the culture one discovers simple piety that is obvious and romantic in its expression. They lived at a time of high linguistic awareness that caused them to be both clever and experimental in their language and to try things in Hebrew that were sometimes in imitation of what was being done in Arabic by themselves and others and that led them to stretch the ancient language beyond its Biblical and Talmudic limits. The results were sometimes merely interesting and sometimes successful at forging memorable expressions of piety and thought.

There were many fine poets in that era. No doubt the leading master of religious expression among them was Jehudah ben Samuel, more commonly known as Judah Halevi. To illustrate the themes of divine grace in his corpus of writings, I begin by citing a poem titled, in translation, Now Cometh the Light as translated by Nina Salaman in SELECTED POEMS OF JEHUDAH HALEVI, edited by Heinrich Brody (New York, 1973).[1]

> Together in Thy light, O God resplendent,
> Do we see light!

The people that walked in darkness--
Their hope how long deferred!--
While biting sin still troopeth at their heel,
Upon them, like clear heat in sunshine,
Shall dwell the light.

With veil on the uncovered head,
With glory in place of rent apparel,
Wilt Thou clothe them; the light, once sown,
    made manifest
Again, as Thou has said: "Let there be light,
And there was light."

Thy banner, over them whose knees stumble,
Upraise and clear the way before them
    by an Angel; and Thou wilt bless
The seed of the upright, what time Thou makest light
Of them that rebel against the light.

While he moaneth like a servant panting after
    the shade,
Do Thou lay the majesty of Thy salvation upon him;
And cry: "How long, O sluggard,
Wilt thou sleep in the house of darkness?   Arise,
shine!
Now cometh the light!"

"Grace, grace," proclaim; and set up two rows
Of olive trees for kindling the lights,
And they shall serve for lamps--
Their oil within the shrine of God resplendent,
For the Light!

The first thing that you, the reader, may have noticed about this poem is the fact that most of its lines are far from original. They are lines from the Bible and the editor, Heinrich Brody, has taken pains to note them for us in the translation as it appears in his book. (For those who care to know them they are, in sequence, Ps. 76:5, Ps. 36:10), Isa. 9:1, Gen. 49:17 & 19, Isa. 18:4, Job 38:19, Ps. 97:11, Gen. 1:3, Mal. 3:1, Job 24:13, Job 7:2, Prov. 6:9, Isa. 60:1, Zech. 4:7 and Zech. 4:3 & 11-14.) The poem is actually a collage of Biblical verses.

Yet the collage itself is original and doing it was an original thing to do. It was also original to work the lines around the central theme of light, a theme likely inspired by the symbolic value of the *menorah* that is obviously referred to in the final stanza of the poem. For the poet, the menorah and light itself were symbolic of divine grace in the manner that was suggested by the prophet Zechariah.

The term here translated "grace" is not the term *hesed* that we noticed in the Talmudic sources above. It is the Hebrew term *hen* that is frequently translated as "compassion." It is a near synonym of *hesed* with less emphasis on the obligatory nature of it and the bond that established the obligation and more emphasis on the quality of the act itself, a quality of concern and tenderness. The poet conceived of God as the One who looks with compassion and acts with concern for His people.

The closing lines of another poem express a notion of divine grace that a Lutheran or Methodist Christian might find quite meaningful.

> And what hath fate for me, if not Thy favor?
> If Thou art not my lot, what is my lot?
> I am despoiled and naked of good works,
> Thy righteousness alone my covering--
> But why make longer speech, why question more?
> O Lord, before Thee is my whole desire.[2]

Such similarity between the thoughts of two traditions, one Jewish and one Christian, leads one to suppose that in all religious traditions, the hymnody expresses the same desires and beliefs.

The centrality of forgiveness as an experience of God's grace can be seen in this next selection.

> Let Thy favour pass to me,
> Even as Thy wrath hath passed;
> Shall mine iniquity for ever
> Stand between me and Thee?
> How long shall I search
> For Thee beside me, and find Thee not?
> O Dweller amid the wings of the Cherubim
> That are outspread over Thine Ark,
> Thou hast enslaved me unto strangers
> While I am the man of Thy right hand.
> My Redeemer! To redeem my multitudes
> Rise and look forth from Thine abiding place.[3]

It is interesting to notice that the estrangement caused by iniquity is equated to the exiled condition of the total people of Israel. In another poem, *Thou Who Knowest Our Sorrows*, this theme is explored more fully. Its opening lines declare the whole theme, a prayer to the One who could bring back the exiles to the symbolic reality of Zion and the Holy Land, to happiness.

> Thou who knowest our sorrows, and bindest up
>   our wounds,
> Turn again our tens of thousands to the land of
>   our abodes.
> There shall we offer our oblations, our vows,
>   our freewill offerings,
> There shall we make before Thee the offerings
>   due to Thee.[4]

A great many of Halevi's poems, including those that are most well known today, are about Zion and his own anticipated return to the land of his ancestors. The land itself was perhaps his own most powerful symbol of divine grace. And that being true for him, it had to be and continues to be true for many if not most other Jewish people. Zion is a graceful word. It is about where God and the seeking mortal can meet.

Nor is the idea strange to non-Jewish people. The idea of sacred place or sacred places is extremely common to humans the world over. It is precisely this that makes pilgrimages the important religious experiences that they can be.

Judah Halevi was a man who earned the label "lover of Zion" because of the many poems he composed around that theme. Yet also because he actually made the pilgrimage journey himself, writing many of his best poems on the way. He journeyed by sea, recording the experience of seasickness along with his longing for the goal of his voyage and landed in Egypt. From there he went overland and, according to popular legend, died at the wailing wall of Jerusalem by being trampled under the hooves of the horse of an Arab cavalryman.

He was a man who lived with an ever increasing and cultivated longing for ever more of the Creator's grace. If ever there was a mortal who lived in anticipation of more and more of that grace, this was that man.

Other Jewish poets of the period and place show their own understanding of the theme of God's grace as well. Solomon Ibn Gavirol is one of the best known. A short example will illustrate.

> When all within is dark,
> And former friends misprise;
> From them I turn to Thee,

And find Love in Thine eyes.

When all within is dark,
And I my soul despise;
From me I turn to Thee,
And find Love in Thine eyes.

When all Thy face is dark,
And Thy just angers rise;
From Thee I turn to Thee,
And find Love in Thine eyes.[5]

The poem may seem too sentimental for the taste of some readers. If this be the case we could advise reading some of the Christian devotional literature of that time and later. Sentimentality was a manner of religious speech that was quite popular then and still is in many circles today. Aside from the sentimentality of the closing lines, one can see a couple of profound insights in the second and third stanzas. While it is common to express the thoughts of stanza one ("if everybody else rejects me I can still turn to You"), it is a matter of some insight to say that one must turn to God when rejected by self and, even more, to turn to God when God seems to be rejecting.

The third stanza of another poem illustrates a thought more commonly expressed, but in eloquent metaphor.

I have sought Thee daily at dawn and twilight,
I have stretched my hands to Thee, turned my face,
Now the cry of a heart athirst I will utter,
Like the beggar who cries at my door for grace.[6]

The reference to daily prayers at dawn and twilight reflect the daily habits of prayer of pious Jewish people.

A third well known poet of the era was Moses Ibn Ezra. The opening stanza of one of his poems illustrates the common human theme of discovering divine grace through forgiveness.

I rose at dawn to praise Thy name,
My sins o'erwhelmed my soul with shame,
But comfort after penance came,

For all my hopes are set in Thee.[7]

Another poem's entirety illustrates the same human experience in words that could just as well have been uttered by a Christian.

O Thou, that graciously attendest
To the voice of suppliants,

and to the sweet words of psalmody,
Bethink Thee of the trustful one
Who knocks at the gates of prayer,
and in the darkness at the dead of night
Whilst the world sleeps,
Cries: "I stand upon my ward
all the night."
Of old, Thou madest Israel like a vineyard--
Wherein Thou didst plant tender vines.
Alas! Thou didst break down his fences,
All they that pass by, hiss at him
Thou hast strengthened the hands of his foes
And destroyed him utterly.
They have stript off his branches
and heaped them up in the road.

Oh, hear the cry of Thy people
And incline unto their plea--
In their misery,
Hide not Thine eyes from their grief!
Oh, hasten their deliverance--
For Thou art their Redeemer--
And cast all their sins
like a stone, into the depths.[8]

As we have seen in other examples of the genre, the language is richly Biblical in its phrases and metaphors. So also is the language of most Christian literature.

Our final example comes from the pen of yet a fourth poet of the era, one Abraham Ibn Ezra.

I hope for the salvation of the Lord,
In Him I trust, when fears my being thrill,
Come life, come death, according to His word,
He is my portion still.

Hence doubting heart! I will the Lord extol
With gladness, for in Him is my desire,
Who, as with fatness, satisfies my soul,
That doth to heaven aspire.

All that is hidden, shall mine eyes behold,
And the great Lord of all be known to me,
Him will I serve, His am I as of old;
I ask not to be free.

Sweet is ev'n sorrow coming in His name,
Nor will I seek its purpose to explore,
His praise will I continually proclaim,
And bless Him evermore.[9]

The poem is titled "Resignation" in the edition I chose. An equally good title might be, "Prisoner of God's Grace."

The fact that these poems were fairly popular in their own time and survived the centuries because of their popularity and the fact that Christian hymnists expressed similar thoughts in the words they wrote indicates that there was and is a common human understanding of divine grace. It is not an experience unique to any one tradition.

As a contrast to the romantic minds of the Sephardic poets we shall now consider the mind of a keen and brilliant philosopher, the incomparable Moses Maimonides. Ben Maimon (the Hebrew form of his name) was a man of the twelfth century (b. 1135, d., 1204), and a man of such fame that he finished his career as court physician to the sultan in Cairo. In his own time he was perhaps known best as a great physician and second best as a great jurist and counsellor. Later ages look back on him as one of the truly great philosophers and scientists of that time.

He was a person of such charity that one could think of him as the very personification of God's grace in a human form. He virtually gave all that he was and had to others. As physician in the Sultan's court he devoted so much time to patients as to allow himself only one meal per day. As jurist and counsellor he allowed Sabbath to be filled with the activity of instruction and study with others. He carried on a considerable correspondence in which he offered his wisdom and counsel to many fellow Jews. As philosopher his books were written for the sake of answering people's questions and solving the intellectual problems that he felt were puzzling his people.

In one of the greatest of his written works, GUIDE OF THE PERPLEXED, he exhibits a profound understanding of the grace of God in the very nature of our being. This excerpt will illustrate.

> If you consider the divine actions--I mean to say the natural actions--the deity's wily graciousness and wisdom, as shown in the creation of living beings, in the gradations of the motions of the limbs, and the proximity of some of the latter to others, will through them become clear to you. Similarly His wisdom and wily graciousness, as shown in the gradual succession of the various states of the individual, will become clear to you. The brain is an example of the

gradation of the motions and the proximity of the limbs of an individual: for its front part is soft, very soft indeed, whereas its posterior part is more solid. The spinal marrow is even more solid and becomes more and more solid as it stretches on. The nerves are organs of sensation and of motion. Accordingly the moves required only for apprehension by the senses or for motion that presents but little difficulty, like the motions of the eyelids and of the jaws, proceed from the brain, whereas the motions required for moving the limbs proceed from the spinal marrow. As, however, it is impossible for a nerve, in view of its softness-- even for a nerve proceeding from the spinal marrow--to move an articulation, the matter was wilily and graciously arranged as follows: the nerves are ramified into fibers, and the latter, having been filled with flesh, become muscles. Thereupon the nerve, having overpassed the extremity of the muscle, having become more solid, and having been commingled with fragments of ligaments, becomes a tendon. The tendon joins and adheres to the bone; and thereupon, because of the gradation, the nerve is capable of moving a limb. I mentioned only this one example to you because it is the most obvious of the wonders explained in the treatise "On the Utilities of the Parts of the Body," all of which wonders are clear, manifest, and well known to those who consider them with a penetrating mind. Similarly the deity made a wily and gracious arrangement with regard to all the individuals of the living beings that suck. For when born, such individuals are extremely soft and cannot feed on dry food. Accordingly breasts were prepared for them so that they should produce milk with a view to their receiving human food, which is similar to the composition of their bodies, until their limbs gradually and little by little become dry and solid.

Many things in our Law are due to something similar to this very governance on the part of Him who governs, many He be glorified and exalted.[10]

To Maimonides, the world was basically a good world. Even natural disasters and pain and suffering were seen within the context of a total goodness in which he believed. He could not escape thinking that there was some kind of judgment on human behavior in the total process but that the end purpose of that judgment is for our benefit. He could not imagine God having any other purpose than a good purpose. He was a believer who believed in the grace of

God. To him, God was merciful and compassionate and that, in turn, demands the same qualities in human behavior.

Though he did not think that God could be known in the sense that objects and phenomena are known, Maimonides insisted that God can be characterized and that nothing characterizes God better than the term merciful. He writes,

> "God, may He be exalted, is said to be merciful, just as it is said, `like as a father is merciful to his children,' and as it says, `I will pity them as a man pities his own son.' It is not that He, may He be exalted, is affected and has compassion. But an action similar to that which proceeds from a father in respect to his child and that is attached to compassion, pity and an absolute passion, proceeds from Him......... And just as when we give a thing to someone who has no claim upon us (This is called grace in our language)..... so is the term applied to Him....... Such instances are frequent. For He, may He be exalted, brings into existence and governs beings that have no claim upon Him with respect to being brought into existence and being governed. For this reason He is called gracious."[11]

In keeping with the idea that the natural order is shot through with the graciousness of God and his observation that this grace is clearly seen in the workings of our own body and intellect, he did not see humans as helpless objects of divine compassion. To the contrary, and in keeping with a strong strain of this emphasis in Jewish religious philosophy, he saw humans as equipped by the grace of God to live through the struggles of life triumphantly.

He particularly saw human intellect as a marvelous gift from the Creator. Intellect itself was a gift of divine grace. With our intellect we can understand what is within our grasp, we can appreciate what is wonderful, we can solve the problems with which we are face from day to day. We must only be careful to recognize that God is the Giver and not presume to think of our intellectual powers as an accomplishment.

Maimonides had a remarkably canny understanding of the human element in sacred scripture. A good portion of his *Guide* is an explanation of the premise that "the Torah speaks in the language of the sons of man" and another good portion on its corollary, "the Torah speaks in exaggerated language." Yet he had profound respect for what he himself called divine inspiration of it. He felt that scripture does reveal something of God and that Moses and all the prophets were uniquely gifted to speak God's will. And in the scriptures as well as in nature he found God to be dominantly good. "Nothing that is evil descends from above," he wrote in quotation of Genesis *Rabbah, LI.*

In fact, so optimistic was he about the eventual good outcome of all that seems bad, that Maimonides was able to focus on the final reward in his interpretation of the classical case of Job (which he conceded to be, at least in part, a "parable"), that he wrote this summary of the case: "God sends down calamities upon an individual, without their having been preceded by sin, in order that his reward may be increased." To Maimonides, grace was the norm of God's dealings. "Wrath" was the exception and only for the sake of further or ultimate grace. He felt that life testified to that. So also did the Torah and all prophetic speech.

A key term in his understanding of the ways of God was the Hebrew term *hesed*. His own explanation of the term follows.

> We have already explained in the Commentary on Aboth that the meaning of *hesed* is excess in whatever matter excess is practiced. In most cases, however, it is applied to excess in beneficence. Now it is known that beneficence includes two notions, one of them consisting in the exercise of beneficence toward one who has no right at all to claim this from you, and the other consisting in the exercise of beneficence toward one who deserves it. In most cases the prophetic books use the word *hesed* in the sense of practicing beneficence toward one who has no right at all to claim this from you. Therefore every benefit that from Him, may He be exalted, is called *hesed.*[12]

The Torah itself, a special gift to Israel, was a demonstration of God's grace or *hesed.* "The Law as a whole aims at two things," he wrote, "the welfare of the soul and the welfare of the body."[13]

The closing words of Part II of his great Guide show how central was the concept of grace in Moses' theological thinking.

> This is the extent of what I thought fit that we should set down in this Treatise; it is a part of what I consider very useful to you. I hope for you that

through sufficient reflection you will grasp all the intentions I have included therein, with the help of God, may He be exalted; and that He will grant us and all Israel, being fellows, that which He has promised us: *Then the eyes of the blind shall be opened and the ears of the deaf shall be unstopped. The people that walked in darkness have seen a great light; they that dwelt in the land of the shadow of death, upon them hath the light shined.*
AMEN

God is very near to everyone who calls,
If he calls truly and has no distractions;
He is found by every seeker who searches for him,
If he marches toward Him and does not stray.[14]

"Iberian Grace," I titled this chapter, perhaps too cutely and cleverly I do admit. What I meant to communicate and demonstrate was that the vibrant Jewish culture of ancient Spain was as vibrantly alive in regard to religion as well as in commerce or science and that its religious awareness was a healthy awareness of the grace of God in the world and in personal lives. Their poets and their greatest philosopher demonstrate that awareness in their own lives and, as their manner of address assumes, in the lives of their fellow Jews.

To the north, in the lands where Latin was the language of both scholarship and religion, other poets and philosophers were sounding similar themes. To them those great themes were Christian realities and they even dared to assume that they were unique to the Christian world. That assumption was wrong, of course. The fact that Jewish and Christian culture were largely at odds with each other in those centuries is a tragic contradiction to that fact human beings within each culture were experiencing and apprehending God's grace in remarkably similar ways.

THE GRACE OF THE GIFTED

To continue our historical quest of the theme of divine grace in Jewish tradition we must move eastward, for when the forces of Christian Spain drove all Jews form the peninsula, the creative spirit moved elsewhere. Here and there in many parts of the world truly creative Jewish people continued to work in a multitude of ways. Yet it was in the east that a communal surge of religious creativity emerged. It was based in part on the kabbalistic tradition of Spain and the book called *Zohar* (Divine Splendor) by Moses de Leon. It flowered in the idyllic hilltop town of Sefat, an upper Galilean lake, Genesaret or Kinnereth, to the south. It was home for many sages and saints. Among the most important were Isaac Luria and Joseph Karo.

When one enters this realm of religion one enters another world of perception. To begin with, this is a tradition that was born out of the otherworldly view of the Kabbalah. The religious quest of the persons within that tradition was a quest for connections --for whatever it is that joins the world below, where we live, with the world above from which all reality emanates.

Continuing from that is a second perception that is often identified with the mind and teachings of Isaac Luria. It is the perception that the world we live in is a broken world that must somehow be put back together. Its reconstruction or reunification is its redemption.

Isaac Luria saw the brokenness itself in a positive way. To oversimplify his thinking about it we can say that, according to Luria, the world is fragmented because God, in the very process of creating it, allowed Himself to explode into trillions of fragments. Those fragments are all about us, of course --in each phenomenon of nature and in our very selves. It is for the believer to see or sense these fragments and "redeem" them by the attention he pays to them. The believers as a group saw this as a task. If they could somehow liberate enough of these "sparks" of divine reality, they could begin a process that would culminate in total redemption. The whole world would again be one. It would be "saved" (to use the favorite Christian term) and the ultimate kingdom of grace would have arrived.

This being true, each devout believer who practiced this way became an important person within God's total plan. It is for that reason that this group of Jewish people, who call themselves the Hasidim, take themselves very seriously. They are the keys to the redemption of all Israel if not all the world.

Jewish Hasidism has entered the awareness of the popular mind thanks to the writings of the religious philosopher, Martin Buber, and the two novelists, Elie Wiesel and Chayim Potok. Both Buber and Wiesel have dealt with the personalities of the tradition itself. Potok has created characters from the living generation of Hasidic Jews who live in New York.

What emerges is a movement that for some reason or other is quite appealing in our time. What the appeal might be is hard to say. It is surely, in part, the fact that the Hasidic tradition focuses on personalities per se and provides us, therefore, with stories that are fascinating to read, be they the complete novels of Potok or the anecdotes of Buber and Wiesel.

Hasidic piety revolved around the gifted personalities known as the *zaddikim*. Each *zaddik* was a sort of saint whose goodness was of benefit to his followers and, to lesser degree, the rest of the world as well. Or, to put it in another phrase, each *zaddik* was a master with his disciples, the *Hasidim*, around him. As the movement developed, it developed as circles with a particular *zaddik*, a holy man, at the center of each. One could even call the movement a cult of the holy man who functioned as a channel of divine grace for the rest.

The tales of these holy ones are the chief literature of the movement. They are tales that dwell on the miraculous or the special wisdom of these righteous ones whom God raised up at time of need.

The time in which the movement appeared was a time of particular need. Baal Shem Tov, the acknowledged father of the movement, whose life spanned the years 1700-1760, appeared at a time when things were not well for the Jews of Eastern Europe. In addition to severe economic and political conditions, there was a spiritual malaise that cried out for help from heaven. The Hasidic masters, the *zaddikim*, were the apparent answer to that cry.

The *zaddikim* were men selected by God to live by severe discipline to redeem the generation in which they lived. To use the jargon of our topic, each *zaddik* was an instrument of God's grace. As that instrument he was at once the humblest and noblest of men. His obedience to God had to be as total as that of a slave yet his bearing had to be that of a prince. Behind all the tales that embellish each of these lives there is the notion of some special divine grace that gifted them to be channels of grace for others.

One could compare them to the saints of the Roman Catholic tradition for there are many points at which the comparison shows similarities. Like the Christian saints they were men of unusual discipline, unusual goodness and merit, unusual humility. In the very telling of a tale of the great master himself, one came to expect this kind of preface: "My teachers, if it pleases you, listen to me and I shall tell you a story of the holy Baal-Shem whose merit strengthens us."

The tale that followed would be a tale of miracles and good deeds.

Scholem Asch, a Jewish author of the century past, produced a novel that portrays the life of a zaddik and the faith of those who looked to such men for wisdom, guidance, healing and comfort. It is the story of a boy who grew to become such a gifted man. In his growing he slowly discovers his gifts yet is always amazed by the fact that he has them. He is a person of profound humility and profound respect for the mystery that uses him as a channel of grace. *The Psalm Jew* is the original title of the novel. In its last publications it is titled *Salvation*. As one reads it one is led into the life of what could be called a Jewish version of St. Francis of Assisi.[1]

Late in the story the chief character (named Yechiel) is brought face to face with human suffering as he is taken to the court of a great rabbi who was fames for his gifts of healing. I quote the scene of the encounter.

"Who are they?" asked Yechiel.

"Can't they see? They are people who are afraid they will find no rest in the next world. That's why they're standing before the Rabbi's door for redemption."

When father and son returned to the House of Study the great room was already filled with dense shadows, so that the worshippers were scarcely discernible. Only the singsong of their voices could be heard. Here and there groups of Chassidim were saying their evening prayer. To cut off the lower part of their bodies from the higher, they had tied belts round their waists and rocked to-and-fro in ecstasy. Other groups sat in the corners listening in the twilight hour to the old men relating legends and miraculous tales. On the long table lay the books of the Law along with volumes of the Talmud, open, but covered with belts, shawls and other objects, for it was the hour of prayer. There was not general service, for the Rabbi was not present; the worshippers prayed singly or in groups as on a day of mourning.

At the top of the table lay an open folio with a shawl covering it. Opposite, against the wall, stood a tall man with back hair and beard shot with gray, his head thrown back. He was praying without moving; his body was as if hewn out of stone. So he stood, like a statue, stretched to his full height in motionless ecstasy. His face with its shut eyes was like an open book turned upward to Heaven. At a little distance stood a group of adoring youths, the disciples of the praying man; they contemplated their master, now rapt up to Heaven, with trembling joy and fear. Boruch-Moishe drew Yechiel's attention to the man by whispering.

"Do you see that man over there? He never moves when he prays. Do you know why? It says in the Bible: `And Aaron did not move from the place.' So he holds that devotion requires no outward sign, but must burn like a flame in the heart of the faithful. Do you know who he is? He's the famous scholar Rab Itche Mayer of Warsaw; the most intimate friend of the Rabbi. If he liked, he could cure everybody we saw in the courtyard by lifting his little finger!"

"Oh, why doesn't he do it then? How can anyone look on the misery of Jews unmoved when he can help it?" asked Yechiel in astonishment.

"That's just what I was about to tell you. Even in such case one must have the strength to control one's impulses. For very often the Evil One assails us through pity. Pity is certainly a good quality, but is must go hand in hand with the Law. If it hasn't justice to support it, it is mere womanish sentimentality."

Yechiel did not venture to contradict this, out of reverence for his father. But his heart was heavy. For he could not understand the ways of these great people.....[1]

As Asch developed the story of the young man Yechiel, he showed him to be true *zaddik* in that he could be moved to pity and could be of help to them in one way or other. And in doing this, Asch was portraying a king of character spoken of in many of the sources as one who could stretch all the way between the realms of bliss and misery to be a true channel of grace for others. There are a number of sources which indicate this, that the ideal *zaddik* is one who goes all the way in his identity with the sufferings of the people. From an excellent source on the entire subject, *The Zaddik*, by Samuel H. Dresner, we drew three excerpts to illustrate the point.In kabbalistic thought, the holy man has a task to perform in relation to the upper spheres and apart from the people. He is the leader of the people, but his destiny is not primarily with them. His primary concern is heaven. He is cast in a cosmological role, moving among the forces of creation, endeavoring to influence the upper spheres to hasten the coming of the messiah.

The zaddik, in contradistinction, must always be understood in relation to the people. He has no completely independent part to play. He stands between heaven and earth, "between God and the people," "just as Moses was the intermediary between Israel and the Holy One, blessed be He." Indeed, through the zaddik, the austere loftiness of heaven and the abject lowliness of earth, the transcendence of God and the humanity of man meet. what seems set apart and unalterably opposed find in him a mediating principle which brings them together. "It is only possible to join together two opposites through a third force." "The zaddik is the foundation of the universe, which is peace, for he joins together two opposites as when one makes peace between a man and his neighbor." Flesh and spirit within man, man and his neighbor between men, and man and God beyond man--with all these the zaddik struggles, striving to join them together; between all these the zaddik makes peace.

We are told that when Jacob dreamed his dream about the angels ascending and descending upon the ladder

which reached to heaven, "the Lord stood beside
him" (Gen. 28:13). The Lord was nearby, reassuring
him and giving him the promise of His presence. So
it is with the zaddik, the Lord's messenger, who
descends the ladder of life in order to raise the
people. "Wherever his descent may lead him, he
must be aware that the Glory of God's Presence is
also there.[2]

In a way that was very real to the people of this tradition, each *zaddik*
was an incarnation of God's grace. He was God's mercy in human form, God's
messenger of redemption.

There is a strong emphasis on God's mercy for sinners in this Hasidic
tradition. A few anecdotes from Buber's *Tales of the Hasidim* illustrate this.

One midnight when Rabbi Moshe Leib was absorbed
in the mystic teachings, he heard a knock at his
window. A drunken peasant stood outside and asked
to be let in and given a bed for the night. For a
moment the zaddik's heart was full of anger and he
said to himself: "How can a drunk have the insolence
to ask to be let in, and what business has he in this
house!" But then he said silently in his hearth: "And
what business has he in God's world? But if God
gets along with him, can I reject him?" He opened
the door at once, and prepared a bed.

The rabbi of Sasov once gave the last money he had
in his pocket to a man of ill repute. His disciples
threw it up to him. He answered them: "Shall I be
more finicky than God, who gave it to me?"[3]

Rabbi Moshe Leib told this story:

"How to love men is something I learned from a
peasant. He was sitting in an inn along with other
peasants, drinking. For a long time he was as silent
as all the rest, but when he was moved by the wine,
he asked one of the men seated beside him: `Tell me,
do you love me or don't you love me?' The other
replied: `I love you very much.' But the first peasant
replied: `You say that you love me, but you do not
know what I need. If you really loved me, you
would know.' The other had not a word to say to
this, and the peasant who had put the question fell
silent again.

"But I understood. To know the needs of men and to
bear the burden of their sorrow--that is the true love
of men."[4]

> The rabbi of Sasov used to visit all the sick boys in the town, sit at their bedside, and nurse and take care of them. Once he said: "He who is not willing to suck the pus from the sore of a child sick with the plague has not climbed even halfway up the mountain to the love of his fellow men."
>
> On the eve of the Day of Atonement, when the time had come to say Kol Nidre, all the Hasidim were gathered together in the House of Prayer waiting for the rabbi. But time passed and he did not come. Then one of the women of the congregation said to herself: "I guess it will be quite a while before they begin, and I was in such a hurry and my child is alone in the house. I'll just run home and look after it to make sure it hasn't awakened. I can be back in a few minutes."
>
> She ran home and listened at the door. Everything was quiet. Softly she turned the knob and put her head into the room-- and there stood the rabbi holding her child in his arms. He had heard the child crying on is way to the House of Prayer, and he had played with it and sung to it until it fell asleep.[5]

The portrayals of the great *zaddikim* that arise out of the many preserved tales are portrayals of men who had uncanny understanding of the compassion of God. The legally trained rabbis of the Talmudic tradition could have the most erudite understanding of the laws of Torah. The *zaddikim* had profounder understanding of God's grace, according to the tales.

The theology underlying all this is a theology well expressed in this paragraph from Dresner's book on the writings of Rabbi Yaakov Yosef of Polnoy, *The Zaddik.*

> God did not forsake the world after having created it. His love for His creation manifests itself in His constant effort to reach down to it. As Sinai His voice broke through the curtain which man had painstakingly erected. Never again was it heard so clearly and so decisively, but the effort on His part to speak to His creatures never ceases. Saintly souls of all ages have caught echoes of the beyond: "A voice goes out from Mount Horeb every day...." this outpouring from heaven to man is called, in kabbalistic terminology, *shefa*, and may be likened to the rays which emanate from the sun, ceaselessly reaching out to brighten the darkness of the world. To receive the spiritual outpouring which endlessly and lovingly flows from heaven and to transmit it to

his people is the task of the zaddik. In this sense the
zaddik is spoken of as a "channel."[6]

The idea of two worlds, a higher and a lower world, that can either be
separate from or in touch with each other, is a basic structure in this theology
and structure that finds its roots in the kabbalistic lore. The basic difference
between the great mystics of the kabbalistic tradition were men who rose to the
heavens and did not come down while the *zaddikim* of Poland's poverty-stricken
world were men who made the connection. Yet not without the ability to
simply take flight when they needed. In the legends of the founder of this
movement, the great Baal Shem Tov, there are many stories about his rapid
journeys in which a carriage drawn by horses can cover incredible distances in
short periods of time, usually at night. The carriage suggests the famed chariot
upon which Elijah ascended without dying. It seemed that this greatest of the
zaddikim lived in a sphere of reality that was somewhat elevated above the
earth, always drawn toward heaven.

Yet his gifted nature, unique as it was, was for the sake of the many.
He was a vessel of grace for the sake of mending the broken vessels.

GRACE IN REFORM

To seek another strand of the theme of divine grace in Jewish tradition we shall now turn to the career and writings of Moses Mendelssohn, a German Jew of the 18th century whose very life, like the life of Moses Maimonides, can be characterized as a graceful life. An irenic and brilliant man, he so inspired the German intellectuals of his day that one of them, the great poet and playwright Gotthold Lessing, saw Mendelssohn as the ideal human of his day, as the Nathan the Wise of his most famous play.

Moses Mendelssohn was a remarkable man. He was something of a prodigy in his scholarly achievements. He was viewed as a veritable saint for his personal life. His literary accomplishments include a fine translation of the Hebrew Bible into German, many tracts, many essays and letters and some books that include what to me is the best of his work, a book titled JERUSALEM. In that book, which is a political philosophy, we meet a wonderfully liberal spirit which epitomized the enlightenment age that he well represents. One quotation from that book may best demonstrate that spirit. I quote from pages 19-20 of the Schocken English edition, translated and edited by Alfred Jospe.[1]

> Which form of government is the best? Until now, a number of contradictory answers-- all of them apparently true-- have been given to this question. Actually the question is too vague, as is a similar question in the medical field, Which food is best for our health? Obviously, each complexion, climate, age, sex, and way of life requires a different answer. The same is true with regard to our politico-philosophical problem. For each people, at each

> stage of their civilization, a different form of government will be best.

One can say that this opinion is far too liberal for the age in which we now live, though it be a full three centuries later.

A basic premise in the thinking of Moses Mendelssohn and some of his contemporaries is that each individual human should be free to be what he or she needs to be, think what he or she needs to think and decide what he or she wants to decide. He felt this was a basic freedom built into creation and therefore a freedom that can be called a gift of God's grace.

This was a freedom that he felt must be respected by governments and even more so by religious institutions and their leaders. Indeed much of his life's energy was consumed in the defense of individuals, especially fellow Jews, whose rights were not so respected. Neither church nor state had the right, as he saw it, to coerce people in any way, be it by reward or punishment, force or bribery. The only right he would grant the highest of human authorities was the right of persuasion, through instruction, teaching, encouragement or motivation (pp. 35-36 of op. cit.). And in matters of interpersonal affairs, he saw no single human as having the right to do more than that with another. His own unfortunate experience at the hands of the Lutheran clergyman, Johann Caspar Lavater, served to demonstrate his convictions on that matter. Lavater had embarrassed Mendelssohn by challenging him in print, without his foreknowledge, to challenge the claim that Christianity was "right" and Judaism "wrong" as religions.

Mendelssohn believed that there was no such thing as a right or wrong religion. Because Judaism was the religion of his heritage, that was the best or "right" religion for him. For Lavater it had to be Christianity and he more than willingly granted the privilege of that conviction to him, but did not concede that Christianity was the only valid religion for all. Mendelssohn was convinced that divine grace operates in any if not all religions and that all men are treated alike by God no matter what their religion. As he understood it, humanity is universal in its needs and in its access to all gifts of the Creator. Indeed, he says as much quite clearly on p. 66 of our version of JERUSALEM.

> According to the tenets of Judaism, all inhabitants of the earth have a claim to salvation, and the means to attain it are as widespread as mankind itself, as

> liberally dispensed as the means of satisfying one's
> hunger and other natural needs.[2]

A more eloquent statement precedes that remark in the source we have chosen to cite. In it one may notice the emphasis on creation and natural order, a consistent Jewish understanding of grace.

> It seems to me that only with regard to historical
> truths did God, in His supreme wisdom, have to
> instruct mankind either by human means..... But the
> eternal truths that are necessary for man's salvation
> and happiness are taught by God in a manner that is
> more fitting for His dignity: not through sounds or
> letters..... but through creation itself in all its inter-
> relatedness, which is legible and intelligible to all
> men. Nor does He confirm these truths by miracles
> which would merely fortify our belief in the
> credibility of certain historical events. Instead, He
> awakens our mind, which He himself has created, and
> gives it an opportunity to observe the inter-relatedness
> of things as well as its own workings and to convince
> itself of those truths which destiny enables man to
> understand in this life on earth.[3]

Mendelssohn felt quite profoundly that God's grace is a universal operation, that no particular religion provides greater access to it than another. Though he dared not make that judgment of other religions, he repeatedly said that Judaism is revealed legislation and not revealed religion-- fully aware of the claims that Christians were making of their religion as the religion revealed for all. To him, religion was a way of life that is basically a matter of ethics and, to him, each of us must be true to our own ethic. What we term grace and salvation are larger matters that dwarf the ways of any single religion.

God's forgiveness toward all was another profound belief of the philosopher. He dedicated several pages of his book, JERUSALEM, to that end and explained that even the laws of God are within that context and given for our happiness and good welfare (pp. 93 ff. of op. cit.). He was especially disturbed by the Medieval idea of retribution in the hereafter and the threat of that as a way of inducing better behavior from people.

These ideas that were eloquently and repeatedly expressed by Moses Mendelssohn in the eighteenth century, the ideas of the universality of divine grace and forgiveness and the primacy of individual freedom within the realm of divine mercy, emerge a hundred years later as basic tenets in Reform Judaism.

This is no accident, of course. Through the Jews of Germany were not ready for the liberal mind of Moses in his own time, the seeds of thought that he planted did bear fruit. The first movements of Reform took place in Germany and it was among the German Jews of America that the movement became the organization.

Reform Judaism developed out of a profound and practical concern for the plight of intelligent Jewish persons who found themselves more and more at odds with the ghetto mentality as they sought to be part of the new world that was emerging around them in central Europe. It was a concern that Jews not be lost from the Jewish tradition simply for the fault of old and inflexible ways. It sought the changes that were possible in the midst of what appeared to be new necessities.

Once the ice had thawed enough to be broken, to try a metaphor, a new current surfaced: a current of legitimately new ideology. If the ways of the Torah could be changed, it suggested, then perhaps the Torah was not the central concern. More and more it appeared that the prophetic portion of the tradition was its core. The second wave of reformers became reformers of thought and not merely changers of custom.

Arthur J. Lelyveld, writing in a 1974 issue of *Judaism*, points out that Reform moved quickly from the goal of merely making life more comfortable for conscientious Jews to the worthier goal of better fulfilling duties. What resulted was a form of Judaism that was "a national, universalist religion with a mission to bring peace and justice to all mankind."[4]

Jacob Neusner, with his characteristically keen insight, has recently described Reform Judaism as messianic in its philosophical base. We quote an excerpt from his book, *Between Time and Eternity*.

> The two most consequential and influential expressions of modern Judaism are the messianic movements of Reform Judaism and Zionism. Reform Judaism stands for those who preserve the religious approach to life, and Zionism speaks in particular to those who do not. What these two massive movements share is a concentration upon the meaning of great events. Reform Judaism and Zionism take with utmost seriousness the history of the modern world, each interpreting that history, those events, in

> its own way, but in common agreeing that the world was changing and moving towards a climax.
>
> Reform Judaism is a phenomenon of man's restless spirit. At its best it is a dynamic faith --and its very dynamism makes it difficult to describe it adequately. Its traditional roots speak of yesterdays; its branches combine the ancient spirit with the special beauty of each new generation. Reform speaks of man's longing for the sure ways of his fathers and at the same time of his own surging and daring struggle for new ways. It is Jewish to the core, although occasional and temporary acceptance of the habits of changing environments may deceive the casual onlooker."[5]

It is not only the "casual onlooker" who sees more than "occasional and temporary acceptance of the habits of changing environments." Perhaps most who care to look carefully will agree that Reform is an exceedingly important form of humanism. In all of its literature and practice, in fact, it has for most of its history been far more humanistic that theistic. Arnold Jacob Wolf, writing in an anthology has noted that classical Reformers say little about God.[6] Yet it is not simply a matter of no interest, for they tended to think of God as the mystery beyond all mysteries and therefore not something to be discussed. "The idea of God belongs to God and not to man," writes Wolf. "Kedushah is always and only Kiddush ha-Shem. Alvin J. Reines, writing in the same essay collection, however, points out that Reform rejected the concept of "theistic absolutism" and says that there is "no definition of `God,' `Jewish,' or `theology'" that can be consistent with the essence of Reform.[7] What needs to be said, in the mind of Reform, is whatever can be said about us. Some excerpts from an essay by Levi A. Olan serve to illustrate this point of view.

> The primary question today is no longer whether or not we can believe in God, but in what sense we can have faith in man.
>
> A certainly more sensible and surely more realistic attitude is for man to confront the possibility of doing with human nature what he has so wonderfully done with nonhuman nature.
>
> We have the tools to enable man to develop the power to control himself and to related himself cooperatively with his fellow man.[8]

68

Reform has been not only humanistic, but characteristically hopeful in its outlook, as several comments already cited have noted. Sometimes, in its apparent ignorance of the darker side of human nature, that hope has appeared to be naive. At other times, it seems to be a profound awareness of the potential of human goodness. In this, it is characteristically Jewish, for it sees the grace of God working in us and through us more than upon us. Such an awareness is articulated well by David Polish.[9]

> I am suggesting that our estrangement becomes all the more intolerable unless we make our peace with the universe. But once we have achieved this, we can turn inward not in flight nor in illusion, but in truth to the place where man meets God most authentically. Here the tension necessarily engendered by the dialectics of reason is shattered. Here God discloses himself in the pathos of the soul. Here God shares man's loneliness. Here prayer is most anguished. Here the moral law makes its greatest demands.
>
> The God who acts within the cosmic process also acts upon the cosmic process.
>
> God is a process within nature that redeems nature.
>
> There are rigid laws in the universe but there is also freedom.

The idea that all humans are legitimately sons and daughters of God is a trademark of Reform thinking. Reform Jews see humanity as being upon earth to represent God himself, no matter how badly. It is as though God and humanity stand in a partnership of grace. Again, Jacob Neusner articulates it well by saying that Reform sees humans as active co-workers with God, endowed with moral freedom and charged with the responsibility of overcoming evil and striving after ideal goals. Humanity's moral vision and moral striving are a kind of revelation of God's grace. Goodness and the thought of goodness are planted in us by the Creator.

Samuel E. Karff, in an essay found in Bernard Martin's anthology, expresses a Reform view of the relationship of his tradition with that of others and, in the process, explains his understanding of diving grace.

> As a Jew, I need not deny that the mystery of divine love and grace is present in the sacred history of my Christian neighbor, and I disavow the implication -- admittedly present in some of my forefather's

utterances-- that God loves me more than him who dwells outside my covenant. I believe in the mystery of election but reject the concept of special love. Nor must I deny that Christian and Jew each has a role in the work of redemption. But even as the sacred history through which the Christian finds personal salvation is not mine, the truth to which he bears witness subtly and at times not so subtly diverges from my own. Each of us anticipates the coming of God's Kingdom; until then we must wait for the decisive arbitration of our conflicting claims.

The Christian gospel is derived from God's revelation in Jesus Christ, the mission of Israel is grounded in the covenant of Sinai. The key to an understanding of my unique Jewish vocation may be found in *the very structure of the covenant itself, for God's relation to Israel is the very paradigm of His covenant with all men.*[10]

For Reform's well known universal concern, a meditation found on p. 185 of *Gates of Prayer* is a convincing demonstration.[11]

Each of us is a battleground for the struggle of sacred with profane. At times the profane seems to win the day. Love and truth are debased. Reason, our chief glory, is turned to evil ends. And in us the divine gift of compassion lies dormant; we fail to feel the anguish of others.

How much we need You, O God, in days of trial! We need faith to live, faith in Your creative power that overcomes chaos and stirs all life toward a new and better world. We seek You, O God: thereby we grow in vision, as we elevate our souls beyond the sordid to the sacred.

Your presence is the light piercing the darkness on our way, lighting our steps, making us see the beauty and worth in all human beings. May our lips and our lives be one in serving You.

There are points of tension and difference between Reform Judaism and the great father of Jewish Enlightenment, the Jewish term for which is *Haskalah.* In many respects Mendelssohn was more daringly liberal than the Reform theorists who came a full century later. He displayed a freedom of mind that is remarkable for any age. On the other hand, he remained orthodox in his personal habits. He felt no need to depart from custom in the keeping of rituals or the practice of his personal ethics. Reform Judaism began with departures from custom and evolved toward theological or philosophical understandings that match those of Mendelssohn.

It is interesting to observe that in the middle of the twentieth century Reform became more conservative in its language of worship and its observance of tradition. One possible reason for this may have been a feeling of kinship with far more conservative Jews who paid with their lives for being Jewish in World War II. One could observe that if a Jew is going to die for being a Jew no matter what, one may as well be conservative as liberal. Such a change is consistent with Reform mentality, of course, for Reform has practiced the privilege of making whatever changes the times demand, be they steps forward or steps back. Beneath all observable changes remain commitments to principle that guide all change.

In Reform, more strongly than in all other branches of Judaism, God's grace is seen as operative in all of nature and in the lives of any who conscientiously seek to do what is right and good. Reform is optimistic in its conviction that God's grace does flow through all creation and through us insofar as we will permit it. There was a phrase in which this optimism, in company with an equivalent optimism among liberal Christians, was somewhat naive. The events of the twentieth century corrected that. Having absorbed that shock, Reform seems to have rediscovered some optimism and now articulates its aspirations in words that are more reflective and profound than before. Those aspirations seems to be convictions about God's grace and the possibility that humanity may still act as the agents of that grace.

GRACE AND THE SAGE

One of the truly great men of modern American Judaism is Abraham Heschel, renowned teacher, lecturer and author. I refer to him here as a sage because that is the single word which seems to best summarize what he became in human and in Jewish tradition. It was his gift of insight, of wisdom, that has endeared him to a world of people who most value that kind of gift.

It is hard to place a man as great as Heschel, for he transcends most categories into which one can put him, but I dare to call him a representative of the conservative half of American Judaism. Judging him by his personal habits one could perhaps call him orthodox. Unlike many orthodox teachers, however, he did not restrict his movements to the circles of Orthodox Jewry. He was a man who mixed with non-Jewish people and became a favorite teacher to more than one Christian. Indeed, so universal was his scope of vision and language of communication that one could even call him a great humanist.

He authored many books. Among them is a book titled GOD IN SEARCH OF MAN and that book deserves to be a document of special interest to this humble study. Its very title suggests the concept of divine grace as many Christians define it. The very idea that it is more true to say that God seeks us than that we seek God, one of the greatest insights of his career, is a perception of the nature of grace that has proven to be very helpful to many Christian theologians, so helpful that this and others of the books of Abraham Heschel have become basic texts or important books in the curricula of Christian seminaries.

In an introduction to Heschel's book, BETWEEN GOD AND MAN, Fritz A. Rothschild has written a succinct biographical introduction that is appropriate to quote at this point.[1]

> Abraham Joshua Heschel is the product of two different worlds. His life and work can perhaps best be understood as an attempt to achieve a creative viable synthesis between the traditional piety and learning of Eastern European Jewry and the philosophy and scholarship of Western civilization. Born in Warsaw, the descendant of a long line of outstanding leaders of Hasidism, he counts among his paternal ancestors the famous rabbi of Apt, Abraham Joshua Heschel, whose name he bears, and Rabbi Dov Ber of Meseritz, the "Great Maggid," the main disciple and successor of the *Baal Shem*, the founder of the Hasidic movement. On his mother's side, he traces lineage to Rabbi Levi Isaac of Berditshev, another famous master of Hasidism.
>
> Growing up in the closed theonomous world of Jewish piety, he gained during the formative years of his childhood and youth two things that are manifest on every page of his published work: a knowledge and an understanding. The *knowledge* of the Jewish religious heritage was acquired through an undeviating attention during most of his waking hours to the study of rabbinical literature. At the age of ten he was at home in the world of the Bible, he had acquired competence in the subtle dialectic of the Talmud, and had also been introduced to the world of Jewish mysticism, the *Kabbalah*. The *understanding* for the realness of the spirit and for the holy dimension of all existence was not primarily the result of book learning but the cumulative effect of life lived among people who "were sure that everything hinted at something transcendent"; that the presence of God was a daily experience and the sanctification of life a daily task. In his book, *The Earth Is the Lord's: The Inner World of the Jew in East Europe*, Heschel has set a lasting memorial to a vanished world - a world vanished in Hitler's gas chambers and concentration camps during the Second World War.
>
> At the age of twenty Heschel, after having prepared himself in Poland for the requirements of modern academic life, left the closed world of traditional life and lore to enroll as a student at the University of Berlin and the *Hochschule für die Wissenschaft des*

Judentums. Although he developed wide cultural and artistic interest, his studies were concentrated mainly in the fields of Semitics and philosophy. The Hochschule appointed its erstwhile student an instructor in Talmud, and the publication of his *Maimonides* (1935), a biography and interpretation of the great medieval philosopher and codifier, established his reputation as a fine scholar, a gifted and imaginative writer, and a master of German prose. Heschel is one of the rare writers who have a distinguished literary style in whatever language they touch. He writes equally well in English, German, Hebrew, and Yiddish. His study on Hebrew prophetic consciousness, *Die Prophetie,* which had earned him a Ph.D. degree at Berlin University, was published by the Polish Academy of Science in 1936 and hailed as an outstanding contribution by leading Biblical scholars.

In 1937 Martin Buber chose Heschel as his successor at the central organization for Jewish adult education and the Judische Lehrhaus. The latter was founded by Franz Rosenzweig in Frankfurt on the Main. There Heschel taught and directed many of the educational activities connected with the last phase of the memorable German-Jewish cultural renaissance that flourished during the Nazi regime only to come to a sudden end with the pogrom of November 10, 1938, and the subsequent extermination policy of the war years.

A mass deportation action in October, 1938, found Heschel himself expelled by the Nazis together with the rest of the Polish Jews resident in Germany. He taught for eight months in Warsaw at the Institute for Jewish Studies, the training school for Jewish teachers and rabbis, before departing for England, where he established the Institute for Jewish Learning in London. In 1940 he received a call from the Hebrew Union College in Cincinnati, where he was Associate Professor of Philosophy and Rabbinics for five years. In 1945 he joined the faculty of the Jewish Theological Seminary of America in New York, where he is Professor of Jewish Ethics and Mysticism.

As is the case with most Jewish religious philosophers, Heschel does not use the word *grace* as a key term. That term and that concept are simply not the starting point in his theological thinking. The term does show up in his writing, however. In a few quotations from the book we have chosen as the basic source for this study, his GOD IN SEARCH OF MAN, one can see the term used in ways that concord with conservative Christian thinking.[2]

> "There is a loneliness in us that hears. When the soul parts from the company of the ego and its retinue of petty concerns; when we cease to exploit all things but instead pray the world's cry, the world's sigh, our loneliness may hear the divine grace beyond all power."

> "The most precious gifts come to us unawares and remain unnoted. God's grace resounds in our life like a staccato."

> "Alone we have no capacity to liberate our soul from ulterior motives. This, however, is our hope: God will redeem where we fail; he will complete what we are trying to achieve. It is the grace of God that helps those who do everything that lies within their power to achieve that which is beyond their power."

Other phrases that crop up here and there also tune closely to what the Christian world has come to know as the grace of God: phrases that use such terms as "mercy," "love" and "forgiveness." On p. 126 of the source we are quoting, Heschel speaks of our quest as for "a Being to whom we may confess our sins," for "a God who loves." On p. 162 we find this remarkable line.

> "Beyond all mystery is the mercy of God. It is a love, a mercy that transcends the world...."

Similarly, on page 353 we read, "Beyond the mind is mystery, but beyond the mystery is mercy. Out of the darkness comes a voice disclosing that the ultimate mystery is not an enigma but the God of mercy: that the Creator of all is the `Father in Heaven.'" On p. 300 we find the remark that "beyond His will is His love."

At other points he speaks of God's "unending love" (p. 290) or uses the phrase, "in the name of God's mercy" (p. 269). And for those Lutherans who like to credit all things to God, a seeming echo of Martin Luther's famous "I cannot by my own reason or strength" appears on page 138.

> "Man's walled mind has no access to a ladder upon which he can, in his own strength, rise to knowledge of God."

There is no way, however in which we can present Heschel's thoughts about the grace of God as a mere duplication of Christian thoughts about the grace of God as a mere duplication of Christian thoughts on the subject. Heschel's understanding of it is Jewish to the core and, we think, representatively Jewish as well. More importantly, to repeat what we have already stated once, the concept of God's grace is not the starting point of his theological thinking.

Heschel's starting point is God Himself and how we must understand that God is ineffably mysterious, or sublime, and quite beyond our understanding. This means, according to Heschel, that faith can only be a response and not a result of successful searching or seeking. A series of quotations will best illustrate what this means in the thought process of Heschel himself.

> Ultimate meaning and ultimate wisdoms are not found within the world but in God, and the only way to wisdom is... through our relationship to God. That relationship is *awe*.......... Awe is itself an act of insight into a meaning greater than ourselves (p. 74).

> The beginning of awe is wonder, and the beginning of wisdom is awe (p. 74). Awe precedes faith; it is at the root of faith (p. 77).

> The glory is the presence, not the essence of God... Mainly the glory manifests itself as a power overwhelming the world (p. 82). The whole earth is full of His glory, but we do not perceive it; it is within our reach but beyond our grasp (p. 83).

> Awe, then, is more than a feeling. It is an answer of the heart and mind to the presence of mystery in all things, an intuition for a meaning that is beyond a mystery, and awareness of the transcendent worth of the universe (p. 106).

> The starting point is the unknown within the known (p. 114).

> Faith does not come into being out of nothing. Faith is preceded by awe (p. 153).

To Heschel, God's awe-inspiring manifestation of His glory is an act of grace, a gracious giving of as much of Himself as our limited sense can apprehend or comprehend. "God is not always silent and man is not always blind," (p. 138) says Heschel in his characteristically fresh turn of a thought. In moments, in events, we do encounter the living God and our responses in those encounters are the beginning points of our faith. God's "appearances" are as questions to which we must give answer (p. 137). These are not in the nature of "experiences" but encounters that we are unable to experience (p. 117).

For the Jewish people as a people, the primary revelation of God's will was the revelation at Mt. Sinai. It was not, to be sure, a revelation of God's essence but, in the revelation of will was the revelation of glory.

> We have never been the same since the day in which the voice of God overwhelmed us at Sinai (p. 167).

> The Bible asserts that man has given himself neither his existence nor his wisdom; that both are derived from the will of God. It teaches us also that certain insights come to us not by the slow process of evolution but by His direct, sudden grant (p. 207).

For the people of the Jewish tradition, God's revelation of His will at Sinai was a gracious gift in which the people received their existence as Jews and also received whatever wisdom was and is their peculiar treasure. The revelation at the Mountain is as primary a revelation of God's grace to Jews as is the cross of Christ to Christians. This grace has the double effect of opening the heart of the human to respond as well as providing that to which one must or can respond.

> It is revelation that makes man capable of receiving revelation (p. 219).

The logic of this is a logic well known to those Christians who teach that faith itself is created by that to which faith responds.

As the thoughts of Heschel unfold in three of his works, GOD IN SEARCH OF MAN (1955), MAN'S QUEST FOR GOD (1954) and ISRAEL: AN ECHO OF ETERNITY (1967), he lays before us several powerful symbols of the grace of God.[3] There is, of course, *Sinai* as the sign of God's revelation to Israel. In connection with that is the *Torah*. There is also *Jerusalem* or Mt. Zion, the *Sabbath* and *Creation* itself.

The idea that the creation is a demonstration of God's grace comes through at several points in GOD IN SEARCH OF MAN.

> In radical amazement, the Biblical man faces "*the great things and unsearchable, the wondrous things without number* (Job 5:9). He encounters them in space and in time, in nature and in history; not only in the uncommon but also in the common occurrences of nature (p. 48).

> The sense of wonder and transcendence must not become "a cushion for the lazy intellect." It must not be a substitute for analysis where analysis is possible; it must not stifle doubt where doubt is legitimate. It must, however, remain a constant awareness if man is to remain true to the dignity of God's creation, because such awareness is the spring of all creative thinking (p. 51).

> To the Biblical man, the beauty of the world issued from the grandeur of God; His majesty towered beyond the breathtaking mystery of the universe (p. 96).

> The Biblical man does not see nature in isolation but in relation to God. "At the beginning God created heaven and earth" --these few words set forth the contingency and absolute dependence of all reality. What, then, is reality? To the Western man, *it is a thing in itself*; to the Biblical man, it is *a thing through God.* Looking at a thing his eyes see not so much form, color, force and motion as an act of God. The world is a gate, not a wall (pp. 97-8).

> Our way of living must not be compatible with our essence as created in the likeness of God. We must beware lest our likeness be distorted and even forfeited. In our way of living we must remain true not only to our sense of the grandeur and mystery of existence (p. 283).

> The idea with which Judaism starts is not the realness of evil or the sinfulness of man but rather the wonder of creation and the ability of men to do the will of God (p. 378).

To put it all into non-Heschelian terms, creation's phenomena are gifts that betray the Giver. They are not only acts, but acts of grace. To be more Heschelian in terminology, we must understand that the Presence of *Shekinah* of God is everywhere and yet to be always met in specific somewheres (ISRAEL: AN ECHO OF ETERNITY, p. 10). Since all that is real derives from God, the most natural realities are all that much purer as evidences of God's self-giving or grace. Therefore it can be said that "beyond all mystery is the mercy of God" (p. 162).

Because the event at Mt. Sinai is a peculiar revelation of God's will and glory to Israel, all that derives from that is symbolic of God's grace. Most directly, this is the Torah and the idea of the covenant implicit in it.

We are taught that God gave man not only life but
also the law (p. 299).

The central Biblical fact is *Sinai*, the covenant, the
word of God. Sinai was superimposed on the failure
of Adam (p. 374).

To the Jew, Sinai is at stake in every act of man, and
the supreme issue is not good and evil but God, and
His commandment to love good and to hate evil; not
the sinfulness of man but the commandment of God
(p. 375).

The God who creates heaven and earth is the God
who communicates His will to the mind of man (p.
143).

Religion begins with a consciousness that something
is asked of us (p. 162).

Torah is a particular guidance system for Jewish people. It is the
Creator's expression of will for that peculiar tribe. But God is not expressing
His will merely for the sake of expressing His will or establishing His authority.
It is for the sake of the preservation of this people that the Will of God is
expressed. The Torah, which embodies this will, is a gift of grace.

Man, in all his frightful power, needs a voice that
says NO (pp. 170-1).

As a person responds to this will of God, it works its way in that person
so that the grace of God becomes manifested through that person's deeds.

We must remember that God is involved in our
doings, that meaning is given not only in the timeless
but primarily in the timely, in that task given here
and now (p. 206).

To be given a sense of meaning is, of course to be given a gift. This
gift, the sense of meaning in life, is given by the gracious gift of the Torah
which assumes that all our deeds can have meaning in the sight of God.

To Heschel, the entire Bible, as an enlarged version of the Torah, is the
same basic symbol of God's grace. Because of this Heschel can speak with
extravagant, even romantic language about the whole Bible.

The Bible asserts that man has given himself neither
his existence nor his wisdom; that both are derived
from the will of God. It teaches us also that certain
insights come to us not by the slow process of
evolution but by His direct, sudden grant (p. 207).

> The soul, we believe, is in need of consecration; to
> achieve that goal we must turn to the Bible. There
> are many literatures, but only one Bible (p. 237).

> The Bible is man's greatest privilege. It is so far off
> and yet so direct, categorical in its demands and full
> of compassion in its understanding of the human
> situation. No other book so loves and respects the
> life of man (p. 239).

> The Bible is an eternal expression of a continuous
> concern: God's cry for many..... (p. 254).

In his interpretation of the prophetic portion of the Bible, Heschel notes
two things predominantly: (1) the harshness of God's judgment and (2)
strengthening power of the promises. More specifically he says:

> We must realize that the harsh passages in the Bible
> are only contained in describing actions which were
> taken at *particular moments* and stand in sharp
> contrast with the compassion, justice and wisdom of
> the laws that were legislated *for all times* (p. 268).

> They had no space, they had no land; all they had
> was time and the promise of a land. Their future
> depended upon God's loyalty to His own promises,
> and their loyalty to the prophetic events was the
> essence of the future (p. 216).

> Abraham challenged the intention of the Lord to
> destroy Sodom. In the name of God's mercy, we too
> have the right to challenge the harsh statements of the
> prophets (p. 269).

It is clear from this last quotation that Heschel viewed the mercy of
graciousness of God as higher than the strictest sense of justice. Once again, a
fitting conclusion is a quotation such as the following.

> ....beyond His will is His love. The Torah was given
> to Israel as a sign of His love. To reciprocate that
> love we strive to attain *ahavat* (= love of) *Torah* (p.
> 300).

A very precise token of God's grace, deriving directly from *Torah*, is
Shabbat.

> What is the Sabbath? A reminder of every man's
> royalty; an abolition of the distinction of master and
> slave, rich and poor, success and failure. To
> celebrate the Sabbath is to experience one's ultimate
> independence of civilization and society, of
> achievement and anxiety. The Sabbath is an

embodiment of the belief that all men are equal and the equality of men means the nobility of men. The greatest sin of man is to forget that he is a prince.

The Sabbath is an assurance that the spirit is greater than the universe, that beyond the good is the holy. The universe was created in six days, but the climax of creation was the seventh day. Things that come into being in the six days are good, but the seventh day is holy. The Sabbath is *holiness in time*.

What is the Sabbath? The presence of eternity, a moment of majesty, the radiance of joy. The soul is enhanced, time is a delight, and inwardness a supreme reward (p. 417).

The land of Israel and, within it, Jerusalem and, within that, Mt. Zion, are felt by Heschel to be powerful symbols of God's grace. The entire content of his book, ISRAEL: AN ECHO OF ETERNITY, exhibits and explains this thought. A series of quotations from that work alone can demonstrate what we have in mind.

Jerusalem is not the first among cities. She is the first among visions............ Her holiness is in her being a place of meeting (p. 30).

There is no joy without Jerusalem, and there is no perception of Jerusalem without the perception of her mystery. What is the mystery of Jerusalem? A promise: peace and God's promise (p. 32).

God had a vision of restoring the image of man. So he created a city in heaven and called it Jerusalem, hoping and praying that Jerusalem on earth may resemble Jerusalem in heaven (p. 32-3).

Jerusalem is a recalling, an insisting and a waiting for the answer to God's hope (p. 33).

Let Jerusalem be a seat of mercy for all men (p. 37).

It is dangerous to regard political affairs as religious events; yet since the time of Abraham we were taught that political affairs are to be understood within the orbit of God's concern (p. 137).

We will never be able to sense the meaning of heaven unless our lives on earth include the cultivation of a foretaste of heaven on earth. This may explain why the promise of the land is a central motif in Biblical history (pp. 146-7).

Because of what the Land of Israel was in ancient Biblical history and because of what it has been in the hope of Jewish people through the centuries, Heschel sees enormous significance in the reestablishment of a Jewish population and the founding of a Jewish state there is in this century.

> The Holy Land, having offered a haven to more than two million Jews..... has attained a new sanctity (p. 113).

> The return to the land is a profound indication of the possibility of redemption for all men (p. 220-1).

> The State of Israel is not the fulfillment of the Messianic promise, but it makes the Messianic promise possible (p. 223).

The use of the word *redemption* here and at other points is significant. It is this word, rather than the word *grace*, which is characteristically used by Jewish people when they speak of what Christians would call the gracious activity of God. Heschel's use of the term is typically Jewish and yet as unique as the ways in which he uses all terms in his rather inimitable manner.

The Jewish idea of redemption has a number of components, some of them paradoxical in nature. On the one hand, it is seen as quite totally the work of God. On the other hand, it is a matter in which God operates through the human and in which, in fact, God relies on the human agent to accomplish it. This reliance on the mortal serves to dignify what is mortal, of course, and thus redeems the very agent of redemption.

> The world needs more than the secret holiness of individual inwardness. It needs more than sacred sentiments and good intentions. God asks for the heart because He needs the lives. It is by lives that the world will be redeemed, by lives that beat in concordance with God, by deeds that outbeat the finite charity of the human heart (296).

> In the light of the Bible, the good is more than a value; it is a *divine concern*, a way of God: all deeds are relevant to Him. He is present in all our deeds (p. 375).

> The world is in need of redemption but the redemption must not be expected to happen as an act of sheer grace. Man's task is to make the world worthy of redemption. His faith and his works are preparation for *ultimate redemption* (p. 380).

Redemption is a process, the process by which God works in or "works" history. It is as though God were waging a war against man's corruption of creation in this way. It is as though God were reclaiming what man is losing.

> ....the moral problem cannot be solved as a moral problem. It must be dealt with as part of the total issue of man. The supreme problem is all of life, not good and evil. We cannot deal with morality unless we deal with all of man, the nature of existence, of doing, of meaning (p. 382).

> Every home can be a temple, every table an altar, and all of life a song to God...... The problem of living begins with the realization that all of us blunder in our dealings with our fellow men..... the way we deal with envy, greed and pride......... The primary task is not how to deal with the evil, but how to deal with the neutral, how to deal with needs (p. 383).

> The dreadful confession, the fact that there is nothing in this world that is not a mixture of good and evil, of holy and unholy, of silver and dross, is, according to Jewish mysticism, the central problem of history and the ultimate issue of redemption (p. 371).

It seems to be that in this matter more than any other, Heschel taps into his own Hasidic tradition. Yet not wholeheartedly, for he criticizes the overemphasis on intention that is often found there and asserts that a good deed is a good deed regardless of its intention and that intention alone accomplishes little.

In a basic and general way, redemption is the act or process of reclaiming the worth of something or someone lest it be lost. A prime example: while in bondage in Egypt the Israelites were of virtually no account. They were but chattel, slaves of a totalitarian state. The exodus that resulted in their freedom was an act of redemption out of which they emerged as a people of worth and note, a people with their own name, their own autonomous destiny, their own special covenant with God.

Heschel sees this kind of act repeated in Israel's history, not least of all in the new birth of the State of Israel. "We live by covenants," writes Heschel (ISRAEL: AN ECHO OF ETERNITY, p. 44) and by that he means that Israel's worth is over and over again declared by God. These repeated declarations are demonstrations of God's process of redemption. This obliges every Israeli and every Jew in a peculiar way.

> Our very existence is a witness that man must live
> toward redemption (ISRAEL: ECHO, p. 134).

In ways that Heschel implies but does not always spell out with examples, this process of redemption seen is Israel's history is the process of all human history.

> We are God's stake in human history. We are the
> dawn and the dusk, the challenge and the test. Israel
> reborn is a renewal of the promise. It calls for a
> renewal of trust in the Lord of History.
>
> History cannot come to an end as long as the promise
> exists (ISRAEL: ECHO, p. 133).
>
> Judaism insists upon the single deed as the instrument
> in dealing with evil. At the end of days, evil will be
> conquered one by one (ISRAEL: ECHO, p. 160).

Let us recapitulate and summarize what we observe in the writings of Abraham Heschel. For Heschel, as for other Jewish writers, words such as *redemption, mercy* and *love* are more characteristic than the term *grace* that is so central and dear to Christians. To a great extent, these Jewish terms mean much the same as the word *grace* and its cognates (*mercy* and *love* often among them). Not exactly the same, of course, but enough the same that one can say both refer to the same reality.

Though many Christian writers would use the *grace of God* as their point of departure, Heschel does not. It is the awesome mystery of God that is the departure point for him. Yet, having begun there, Heschel can say in repeated emphases, "beyond the mystery is the mercy." This can only mean that, to Heschel, the *mercy* (or *grace*) of God is truly primary -- that mercy (or *grace*) is even deeper than justice or mystery itself.

What Heschel does point out very explicitly -- and other Jewish writers do the same -- is that God's activity in both nature and in human history is redemptive activity in which the worth or dignity of all parts of creation are dear and declared to be of great value. It is for the sake of His creation and His creatures that God acts and this activity is what Heschel calls the *love* of God.

The signs or symbols of this for Heschel are, of course, not the signs and symbols that are central to the Christian world. While to Christians the grace of God is seen best or only through Christ, the cross and resurrection, the church and the sacraments, for Heschel the Jew the symbols are creation itself, the Sinai encounter with its covenant and the Torah, the Sabbath, the Holy Land of Israel with Jerusalem and Mt. Zion.

Do the Christian and the Jew receive the same reality through two separate sets of symbols?

Whether or not that be so, Heschel sees no separate concerns in Christianity and Judaism. In ISRAEL: AN ECHO OF ETERNITY he spells it out well.

> The climax of our hopes is the establishment of the kingship of God, and a passion for its realization must permeate all our thoughts. For the ultimate concern of the Jew is not personal salvation but universal redemption. Redemption is not an event that will take place all at once at "the end of days" but a process that goes on all the time. Man's good deeds are single acts in the long drama of redemption, and every deed counts. One must live as if the redemption of all men depended upon the devotion of one's own life. Thus life, every life, we regard as an immense opportunity to enhance that good that God has placed in His creation. And the vision of a world free of hatred and war, of a world filled with understanding for God as the ocean is filled with water, the certainty of ultimate redemption, must continue to inspire our thought and action (pp. 160-161).

Heschel's reference to a concern for "personal salvation" is a reference to what he quite properly sees as the major stress in modern Christianity. Though many Christians may take exception to that and feel much more like agreeing with Heschel's Jewish way, the truth of the matter is that Christianity focuses on the individual soul as it speaks of the primacy of the grace of God. Judaism, in its use of the term *redemption*, focuses on the totality of our existence and on the universe itself.

GRACE IN MEETING

One of the most truly universal Jewish personalities was the great twentieth century religious philosopher, Martin Buber. Though he is most famous for one of his earliest literary works, he authored many books and articles that in one way or another show his understanding of the grace of God. In one of those books, TWO TYPES OF FAITH, he did a serious critique of European Christian understanding of religious faith (mostly northern European and Lutheran) that accuses Christians of being too intellectual in their understanding of faith and asserts that Judaism understands it in more personal terms, as "faithfulness to" whatever God is or reveals of Self rather than intellectual "assent to" certain creeds, dogmas or doctrines.

While one can appreciate the keen insights in that book, one may have to say that what he wrote in it concerns two sets of people in any one religious tradition, Judaism as well as Christianity or any other, rather than one tradition as over against another. Putting that aside for the sake of this discussion, one of the important points of the book is that faith is a response to God's approach, a response to divine grace.

Life as response is a central insight and theme is his most well known and earlier work, ICH UND DU (usually translated as I AND THOU). There he begins by spelling out two modes of living, one he refers to as *ich und du* ("you and I"), the other as *ich und es* ("I and it").

The *ich und du* mode of living is characterized by a personal response that says "you" to the reality that meets us. The *ich und es* mode is a life in which one seeks to manipulate or control the realities around us.

Applying this to the realm of religion and connecting it to his thoughts in TWO TYPES OF FAITH, "you" (or "You") is what I must say to God whenever and however God meets me. God cannot be either manipulated or controlled. God can only be met and one's response must be to That which is infinitely beyond manipulation or control. One cannot effectively or adequately talk about God, according to Buber. One can only talk *to* God, truly religious language is the language of prayer.

One can, on the other hand, talk about creeds, doctrine and dogmas. One can even control and manipulate them. One can, after all, write or revise those so-called statements of faith. Such talk is talk in the realm of "I and it" and when we begin to think that it is actually talk about God, we are guilty of arrogance and presumption, or what the Greeks called *hubris*.

Very much in keeping with the Hasidic tradition and especially some of the insights of Isaac Luria, Buber believed that God comes at us, so to speak, in millions of guises. The mysterious "you" of the universe "comes" to us in all that lives and moves around us, whether it be the world of flora and fauna or the world of humans. Each true and honest meeting is an opportunity to respond to the greater You that moves all lesser yous into our presence.

This "coming," this approach toward us, is the essence of Buber's understanding of grace, it seems to me. We cannot control that coming in any way, nor can we stop it. We can fail to sense it, we can even try to refuse to sense it, but we cannot stop it. We must respond or fail to respond.

The response can be a response of anger. It need not be a response of love or devotion in order to be a legitimate response. Anger is a face to face confrontation with what cannot be manipulated or controlled. Indeed, it manifests itself as anger precisely because it cannot manipulate or control the other. More happily the response is a positive response: the you response of prayer, for prayer is the saying of You to God. Whatever the response be, positive or negative, the response itself is somehow created by that which confronts me. Without the confrontation the response cannot be. Martin Buber the Jew came off agreeing with Martin Luther the German on that point: that faith itself is the gift of the Creator.

As Buber understood it, all of God's manifold approaches are approaches of grace, be they approaches for judgment or mercy, reprimand or encouragement, pain or comfort, humiliation or exaltation. The point of it all is to put me into relationship in order that I will live life in relationship and be the kind of I who says You.

I take this insight of Buber's to be the center of the Jewish understanding of divine grace. As Jewish people recite their own history, and they do that often and in many ways, they are reciting a history in which God continually comes --to lead Abraham from Ur to Canaan, to lead Jacob from Canaan to Egypt, to lead the generation of Moses out of Egypt, to lead the tribes into their various territories, to lead Israel and Judah into exile, to lead exiles back to Jerusalem, to lead later generations into diaspora, etc. From here to there they are led but wherever they go they meet God, sometimes as an enemy and sometimes as a friend. Wherever they go they must respond to the mysterious You of their history. Their story is a story of confrontation and the confrontations are of God's design, not theirs. God is the mover. God's actions are primary. They respond with faith or unfaith but it is difficult to avoid responding. Divine grace drives them, pursues them, sustains them. In good times and bad they live by that grace.

Now, having said this about Jews, does one not have to say it about all? Is this not the plight of all humans on earth? Who but God brings us all into being? Who but God has provided and continues to provide the basic environment in which we live? Who but God provides neighbors for us to meet? Who but God meets us in all meetings? What is true for the Jew must surely be true for the rest of us.

It is not particularly Christian to look at it that way, even though a Christian may acknowledge the truth of it. It is more typically Christian to view the world as having a problem that is solved by God's coming, and to see that coming as focussed in the coming of Christ. Christ is God's incarnation, according to Christians. Jesus Christ is God's approach to the world and it is to that precise coming that our response must be directed. That is the narrowness of the Christian understanding of God's coming to us.

Yet within that narrowness the Christian must agree with the Jew that the coming is all God's, that it is God who first approaches us and leaves us no option other than response. In this the Christian and the Jew must share an understanding of grace. Grace is God coming to us. Grace is God's first move. Grace is primary.

The question is the narrowness of the Christian conception and whether it needs to be that narrow.

As the New Testament evangelists recorded the stories of Jesus they consistently recorded that he and his prophetic partner John announced the coming of God's rule or kingdom. Indeed, one can even go so far as to say that the two of them personified that divine rule of God. That was their conviction; that was their cause. But was Jesus himself the sole channel of God's coming? There is not sufficient evidence to sustain that view.

Jesus did seem to view such natural things as bread yeast and birds and blossoms and celestial demonstrations as signs of God's coming. And he did preach that the neighbor who approaches us with need of food, water, warmth or companionship is the coming of God in disguises. Whatever our response to the least of these, according to the Galilean, is our response to God.

It is not hard to put that together with the philosophy of Martin Buber or the teachings of Isaac Luria and his hasidic followers. Jesus the Jew was not greatly unlike other Jews in his understanding of God's coming to us.

We Christians often tell ourselves to return to Christ or to the Bible. Perhaps what we need to do is return to the faith and understanding of Jesus which was, after all, faith in God and not in himself. In such a return we may find ourselves more at one than at variance with our Jewish brothers and sisters. Together we rely on the grace of God. Perhaps we can even learn to understand it together.

NOTES

Notes to chapter one, THE GRACE OF SABBATH

1   See Millgram, Abraham E., SABBATH: THE DAY OF DELIGHT (Philadelphia, Jewish Publication Society, 1944).

2.   Eisenstein, J. K., HERITAGE OF MUSIC (New York, Union of American Hebrew Congregations, 1972).

3.   LUTHERAN BOOK OF WORSHIP, prepared by the churches participating in the Inter-Lutheran Commission on Worship (Minneapolis, Augsburg Publishing, and Philadelphia, Board of Publications Lutheran Church in America, 1978).

4.   Heschel, Abraham, GOD IN SEARCH OF MAN (New York, Harper and Row, 1966), both quotations from p 418.

5.   Seidman, Hillel, THE GLORY OF THE JEWISH HOLIDAYS, Zahasky, M., Ed. (New York, Shengold Publishers, Inc., 1988), p 45.

6.   From Millgram, *op. cit.*, pp 91-95, for this and also for the rest of the service material for *havdalah*.

Notes to chapter two, THE GRACE OF FORGIVENESS

1.   These are taken from the Rosh Hashanah morning service, using various versions and sources as I hope to illustrate only with what seems familiar to Jewish participants.

2.   Barish, Louis, HIGH HOLIDAY LITURGY (New York, Jonathon David Publishers, 1959), pp 167-8.

3.   Chagall, Bella, FIRST ENCOUNTERS (New York, Schocken, 1983).

4.   Agnon, S. Y., DAYS OF AWE (New York, Schocken, 1948), pp 276-7.

Notes to chapter three, THE GRACE OF SACRED SEASONS

1.   The illustrations are taken from various versions of the Hagadah. The Author is accustomed to conducting such a service for his beginning students in a course on Judaism taught at Luther College in Decorah, Iowa, and has developed a version drawn from various sources.

2. Kohler, Kaufman, JEWISH THEOLOGY (New York, Macmillan, 1918), p 62.

3. The translation is from the Writings volume of TANAKH (Philadelphia, The Jewish Publication Society of America, 1982).

Notes to chapter four, THE GRACE OF TORAH

1. See Goodman, Philip, THE SUCCOTH AND SIMHAT TORAH ANTHOLOGY (Philadelphia, The Jewish Publication Society of America, 1984), p 103.

2. See Chagall, *op. cit.*, p 73.

3. As recalled by the author from his own confirmation training more than forty years ago.

4. The translation is from the The Writings volume of TANAKH, *op. cit.*

Notes to chapter five, GRACE IN RABBINIC TRADITION

1. The author started with Herford's PIRKE AVOT (New York, Schocken, 1962) and A RABBINIC ANTHOLOGY by Montefiore and Loewe (London, Macmilland Co., Ltd., 1938). He also consulted Solomon Schechter's RABBINIC THEOLOGY: MAJOR CONCEPTS OF THE TALMUD (New York, Schocken, 1960 ed.) as a guide.

Notes to chapter six, IBERIAN GRACE

1. This edition includes the Hebrew texts on one side with the English translations of Nina Salaman on the other.

2. *Op. cit.*, pp 87-9.

3. *Op. cit.*, p 109.

4. *Op. cit.*, p 106.

5. The translation is from Millgram, Abraham E., ed., AN ANTHOLOGY OF MEDIEVAL HEBREW LITERATURE (New York, Abelard-Schuman, 1961), p 5.

6. *Ibid*, p 6.

7. *Ibid*, p 37.

8. *Ibid*, p 38.

9.   *Ibid*, p 47.

10.   Maimonides, Moses, GUIDE OF THE PERPLEXED, tr. by Shlomo Pines (Chicago, Univerisity of Chicago Press, 1963).

11.   *Op. cit.*, p 125.

12.   *Op. cit.*, pp 630-1.

13.   *Op. cit.*, p 510.

14.   *Op. cit.,* p 638.

Notes to chapter seven, GRACE OF THE GIFTED

1.   Asch, Scholem, SALVATION, tr. by Willa and Edwin Muir (New York, Schocken, 1968), pp 234-5.

2.   Dresner, Samuel H., THE ZADDIK: THE DOCTRINE OF THE ZADDIK ACCORDING TO THE WRITINGS OF RABBI YAAKOV YOSEF OF POLNOY (New York, Schocken, 1974), pp 240-2.

3.   Buber, Martin, TALES OF THE HASIDIM, tr. by Olga Mark (New York, Schocken, 1948), p 85.

4.   *Op. cit.,* p 86.

5.   *Op. cit.,* p 87.

6.   Dresner, *op. cit.,* p 125.

Notes to chapter eight, GRACE OF REFORM

1.   Mendelssohn, Moses, JERUSALEM, tr. and ed. by Alfred Jospe (New York, Schocken, 1969), pp 19-20.

2.   *Op. cit.,* p 66.

3.   *Op. cit.,* p 65.

4.   Lelyveld, J. Arthur, 'Reform Judaism: An Insider's Evaluation," in JUDAISM 89:23:1 (New York, American Jewish Congress, 1974), pp 30-8. The citation is from p 34.

5.   Neusner, Jacob, BETWEEN TIME AND ETERNITY: THE ESSENTIALS OF JUDAISM (California, Dickenson Pub. Co., 1975), p 129.

6. Morton, Bernard, ed., CONTEMPORARY REFORM JEWISH THOUGHT (Chicago, Quadrangle, 1968), p 43.

7. *Op. cit.*, p 62.

8. *Op. cit.*, p 33.

9. *Op. cit.*, pp 50, 57, 58.

10. *Op. cit.*, pp 173-4.

11. GATES OF PRAYER, (New York, Central Conference of American Rabbis, 1975), p 185.

Notes to chapter nine, GRACE AND THE SAGE

1. Heschel, Abraham, BETWEEN GOD AND MAN, ed. by F. A. Rothschild (New York, The Free Press, 1959).

2. GOD IN SEARCH OF MAN (New York, Harper & Row, 1955), pp 140, 142, 407.

3. MAN'S QUEST FOR GOD (New York, Scribner, 1954) and ISRAEL: AN ECHO OF ETERNITY (New York, Farrar, Strauss, & Giroux, 1969).

Bibliography of Works Cited or Consulted

Abraham, I., STUDIES IN PHARISEEISM AND THE GOSPELS, Studies ed. by Harry M. Orlinsky (New York, KTAV, 1967).

Asch, Scholem, SALVATION, tr. by Willa and Edwin Muir (New York, Schocken, 1968).

Barish, Louis, HIGH HOLIDAY LITURGY (New York, Jonathon David Publishers, 1959).

Bronstein, Herbert, ed., A PASSOVER HAGGADAH (New York, Central Conference of American Rabbis, 1974).

Buber, Martin, I AND THOU, tr. by R. G. Smith (New York, Charles Scribner's Sons, 1958)
    I AND THOU, tr. by Walter Kaufman (New York, Scribners, 1970).
    TALES OF THE HASIDIM, tr. by Olga Mark (New York, Schocken, 1948)
    BETWEEN MAN AND MAN, tr. by R. G. Smith (London, Collins, 1964)
    THE KNOWLEDGE OF MAN: SELECTED ESSAYS, tr. by M. Friedman and R. G. Smith (New York, Harper and Row, 1965)
    HASIDISM AND MODERN MAN, tr. by Maurice Friedman (New York, Harper & Row, 1966)
    A BELIEVING HUMANISM, tr. by Maurice Friedman (New York, Simon & Schuster, 1967).

Chagall, Bella, FIRST ENCOUNTERS, tr. by Barbara Bray (New York, Schocken, 1983).

Danby, D. D., THE MISHNAH (London, Oxford University Press, 1933).

Donlin, H. H., TO BE A JEW: A GUIDE TO JEWISH OBSERVANCE IN CONTEMPORARY LIFE (New York, Basic Books, Inc., 1972).

Dresner, Samuel H., THE ZADDIK (New York, Schocken, 1974).

ENCYCLOPEDIA JUDICA (New York, Macmillan, copyright by Keter Pub. House, Ltd., 1971).

Eisenstein, J. K., HERITAGE OF MUSIC (New York, Union of American Hebrew Congregations, 1972).

Fine, Lawrence, tr., SAFED SPIRITUALITY (New York, Paulist Press, 1984).

GATES OF FORGIVENESS: THE UNION SELICHOT SERVICE (New York, Central conference of American Rabbis, 1980)

GATES OF REPENTANCE: THE NEW UNION PRAYERBOOK FOR THE DAYS OF AWE (New York, Central Conference of American Rabbis, 1978).

GATES OF PRAYER (New York, Central Conference of American Rabbis, 1975).

GATES OF THE HOUSE: THE NEW UNION HOME PRAYERBOOK (New York, Central Conference of American Rabbis, 1977).

Goldin, Judah, THE SONG AT THE SEA (New Haven, Yale University Press, 1971).

Goodman, Philip, THE ROSH HASHANAH ANTHOLOGY (Philadelphia, The Jewish Publication Society of America, 1973).
    THE YOM KIPPUR ANTHOLOGY (Id., 1971).
    THE PASSOVER ANTHOLOGY (Id., 1973).

Glazer, Nathan, AMERICAN JUDAISM (Chicago, University of Chicago Press, 1957 & 1972).

Guttman, Alexander, RABBINIC JUDAISM IN THE MAKING (Detroit, Wayne State University Press, 1970).

Herford, R. T., THE PHARISEES (Boston, Beacon Press, 1962).

Herford, R. T., PIRKE AVOT. THE ETHICS OF THE TALMUD: SAYINGS OF THE FATHERS (New York, Schocken, 1962).

Heschel, Abraham, THE SABBATH: ITS MEANING FOR MODERN MAN (New York, Farrar, Strauss & Young, 1951)
    MAN'S QUEST FOR GOD (New York, Scribner, 1954)
    BETWEEN GOD AND MAN, ed. by F. A. Rothschild (New York, The Free Press, 1959)
    GOD IN SEARCH OF MAN (New York, Harper & Row, 1966)
    ISRAEL, AN ECHO OF ETERNITY (New York, Farrar, Strauss & Giroux, 1969)
    THE CIRCLE OF THE BAAL SHEM TOV (Chicago, University of Chicago Press, 1985).

Hoffman, Lawrence, A., GATES OF UNDERSTANDING: APPRECIATING THE DAYS OF AWE (New York, Central Conference of American Rabbis, 1984).

Inter-Lutheran Commission on Worship, LUTHERAN BOOK OF WORSHIP (Minneapolis, Augsburg Publishing House, and Philadelphia, Board of Publication, Lutheran Church in American, 1978).

Kaplan, M. M., Kohn E. and Eisenstein, I., THE NEW HAGGADAH FOR THE PESAH SEDER (New York, Behrman House, 1942).

Kohler, Kaufman, JEWISH THEOLOGY (New York, Macmillan, 1918).

Kravitz, Nathanael, 3000 YEARS OF HEBREW LITERATURE (Chicago, The Swallow Press, 1972).

Ledyveld, J. Arthur, "Reform Judaism: An Insider's Evaluation," JUDAISM 89:23:1 (New York, American Jewish Congress, 1974), pp 30-38.

Maimonides, Moses, GUIDE OF THE PERPLEXED, Pines, Shlomo, tr., (Chicago, University of Chicago Press, 1963).

Matt, Daniel C., tr., ZOHAR: THE BOOK OF ENLIGHTENMENT (New York, Paulist Press, 1983).

Mendelssohn, Moses, JERUSALEM, Jospe, Alfred, ed. and tr. (New York, Schocken, 1969).

Millgram, Abraham E., ed., AN ANTHOLOGY OF MEDIEVAL HEBREW LITERATURE (London, New York and Toronto, Abelard-Schuman: Ram's Horn Books, 1961).
    SABBATH: THE DAY OF DELIGHT (Philadelphia, Jewish Publication Society, 1944).

Mintz, Jerome R., LEGENDS OF THE HASIDIM (Chicago, University of Chicago Press, 1968).

Montefiore, C. J. G. and Loewe, H., A RABBINIC ANTHOLOGY (London, Macmillan & Co., Ltd., 1938).

Morton, Bernard, ed., CONTEMPORARY REFORM JEWISH THOUGHT (Chicago, Quadrangle, 1968).

Neusner, Jacob, BETWEEN TIME AND ETERNITY: THE ESSENTIALS OF JUDAISM (California, Dickenson Pub. Co., 1975)
    TORAH: FROM SCROLL TO SYMBOL IN FORMATIVE JUDAISM (Philadelphia, Fortress Press, 1985).\
    THE MISHNAH, A NEW TRANSLATION (New Haven, Yale University Press, 1988).

Newman, Louis, I., HASIDIC ANTHOLOGY (New York, Schocken, 1963).

PASSOVER HAGGADAH as designed by Rabbi Z. Harry Gutstein and revised by Rabbi Nathan Goldberg (New York, KTAV Publishing House, Inc., 1949).

Petuchowski, Jacob J., PRAYERBOOK REFORM IN EUROPE (New York, World Union for Progressive Judaism, 1968).

Raphael, Chaim, A FEAST OF HISTORY: PASSOVER THROUGH THE AGES AS A KEY TO JEWISH EXPERIENCE (New York, Simon & Schuster, 1972).

Rappaporet, Angelos S., MYTH AND LEGEND OF ANCIENT ISRAEL (New York, KTAV Publishing House, Inc., 1966).

Rivkin, Ellis, A HIDDEN REVOLUTION (Nashville, Abingdon, 1978).

Rosenzweig, Frank, THE STAR OF REDEMPTION, tr. by William W. Hallo (New York, Holt, Rinehart & Winston, 1970).

Salaman, Nina, tr., SELECTED POEMS OF JEHUDAH HALEVI, Henirich Brody, ed. (New York, The Schiff Library of Jewish Classics, 1973).

Schechter, Solomon, RABBINIC THEOLOGY: MAJOR CONCEPTS OF THE TALMUD (New York, Schocken, 1960 ed.).

Scholem, Gershom G., KABBALAH AND ITS SYMBOLISM, Manheim, Ralph tr., (New York, Schocken, 1965).

Scholem, Gershom G., MAJOR TRENDS IN JEWISH MYSTICISM (New York, Schocken, 1973).

Seidman, Hillel, THE GLORY OF THE JEWISH HOLIDAYS, ed. by Moses Zahasky, (New York, Shengold Publishers, Inc., 1988).

Silver, Arthur M., PASSOVER HAGGADAH: THE COMPLETE SEDER (New York, Menorah Publishing Co., 1980).

Stitskin, Leon D., STUDIES IN TORAH JUDAISM (New York, Yeshiva University Press, KTAV Publishing House, 1969).

THE TALMUD, 18 volumes translated under the editorship of I. Epstein (London, Soncino Press, 1948).

Twersky, Isadore, tr. & ed., A MAIMONIDES READER (New York, Behrman House, Inc., 1972).

THE WRITINGS: A NEW TRANSLATION OF THE HOLY SCRIPTURES ACCORDING TO THE MASSORETIC TEXT, third section (Philadelphia, The Jewish Publication Society of America, 1982).